BOOKTIME! PEOPLE

Literature-Based Thematic Units

Preschool–Kindergarten

Written by:
Sue DeRiso, Lisa Kelly, Suzanne Moore,
Mary Nethery, Mackie Rhodes

Edited by:
Ada Goren
Kim T. Griswell

Illustrated by:
Pam Crane, Teresa R. Davidson, Theresa Lewis Goode, Nick Greenwood,
Clevell Harris, Susan Hodnett, Sheila Krill, Greg D. Rieves,
Becky Saunders, Barry Slate

Cover designed by:
Nick Greenwood

www.themailbox.com

©2000 by THE EDUCATION CENTER, INC.
All rights reserved.
ISBN #1-56234-375-0

Manufactured in the United States

10 9 8 7 6 5 4 3 2 1

TABLE OF CONTENTS

FRANKLIN'S NEW FRIEND

Written by Paulette Bourgeois
Illustrated by Brenda Clark

Franklin isn't so sure about Moose, but he soon learns that friends can be different and still have fun together!

READING CIRCLE

Gather your little ones with this musical invitation, sung to the tune of "Pop Goes the Weasel."

> Come and meet a great big moose
> And a little turtle.
> You will see how they make friends
> In our reading circle.
>
> Join me now; we'll read a book
> About a newfound friendship.
> I know you'll want to take a look
> In our reading circle.

(Repeat until all your students have joined their friends in the reading area.)

Once your youngsters have gathered in your group area, read aloud *Franklin's New Friend*.

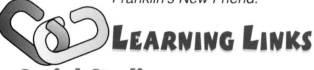

LEARNING LINKS

—Social Studies

Explore diversity with this "egg-citing" idea! In advance, collect a few different types of eggs, such as a small white egg, a large white egg, and a brown egg. Point out that Franklin does not want to be friends with Moose at first because he seems so different. Then show youngsters the eggs, and discuss the differences in size and color. Gently crack each egg into a separate clear glass bowl. Explain to your students that although the eggs looked different on the outside, they are all the same inside. Guide them to understand that people can also look very different on the outside but be very much alike on the inside, with similar feelings and interests.

We are all the same inside!

Create a visual reminder of this idea with this project. Give each child two same-sized white egg cutouts. Have her decorate one cutout with her choice of art materials, such as markers, glitter, buttons, or tissue paper scraps. Then show her how to cut a jagged "crack" across the center of the cutout to divide it into two pieces. On the second egg cutout have her glue a red construction paper heart and then copy this message: "We are all the same inside!" Help her connect the three pieces with a brad on the left side as shown. Encourage youngsters to take these projects home to share with their families and to spark discussions about diversity and friendships.

ART SMARTS

These terrific turtles will be reminders to little ones that making friends means making an effort to be nice. To make one, have a child paint one side of a white paper plate with brown tempera paint. Have her glue four 1¹/₂-inch green construction paper circles to the underside of the plate to resemble the turtle's legs. Then direct her to glue two small wiggle eyes onto a slightly larger green circle and draw a friendly smile to complete the turtle's head. Have her glue the head to one end of a 1" x 4" strip of green paper. Help her accordion-fold the strip before she glues it to the back of the plate to resemble the turtle's neck. Have her add a small green triangle tail to complete her turtle. Display the finished projects on a bulletin board with the title "Stick Out Your Neck for a Friend!"

STORYBOOK CAFÉ

Franklin shares cookies with his new friend, Moose. Encourage each of your youngsters to follow Franklin's example by making two of these cookies and sharing one with a friend.

Turtle Cookies

Supplies:
craft sticks
napkins

Ingredients:
small, round sugar cookies
green-tinted frosting
raisins
green M&Ms® candies

To make one turtle cookie:
1. Use a craft stick to spread green frosting on a cookie.
2. Use dabs of frosting to attach four raisins for legs.
3. Use a dab of frosting to attach a green M&M's candy for a head.

PURPOSEFUL PLAY

What better way to explore diversity in friendships than to play a childhood game from another culture? This Mexican favorite—*piñata*—is a fun choice! To make a friendship piñata, have each child help a friend to paint one of his hands with the paint color of his choice. Have each child make a handprint on a paper grocery bag. Fill the bag with a variety of small treats, making sure the treats can be divided equally among your students. Fold the bag closed; then punch a hole through the folded layers. Thread a strong piece of string through the hole and then use it to suspend the bag from your classroom ceiling.

Before the fun begins, tell students how many treats each of them may collect once the bag is opened. Remind them that a good friend isn't greedy, always shares, and never pushes or shoves. Then have little ones stand back and create a large open area below the piñata. Blindfold one child at a time and give him an opportunity to swing a plastic bat or broomstick at the bag. Continue until the bag is either broken open or knocked down. Have each child gather the designated number of treats. Further focus on friendship by encouraging each child to share (trade) one of his treats with a friend.

TOGETHER

Written by George Ella Lyon
Illustrated by Vera Rosenberry

When friends work together, they can do nearly anything!

  ## READING CIRCLE

Invite your students to storytime by singing this song to the tune of "If You're Happy and You Know It."

> If you'd like to read together,
> Come sit down.
> If you'd like to read together,
> Come sit down.
> If you'd like to read *Together*
> 'Bout a friendship built forever,
> If you'd like to read together,
> Come sit down.

(Repeat the song until all your youngsters are together in the reading circle.)

Once everyone is settled in for storytime, read *Together* aloud.

 ## LEARNING LINKS

—Language Arts

Create a visual reminder of all the wonderful things friends can do together when you make Friendship Wheels. In advance, photocopy page 7 for each child. Have a child cut out both patterns, including the opening on the top wheel indicated by the dotted lines. Ask her to complete each sentence on the bottom wheel and to add an illustration to the space above it. Have her color the friends on the top wheel. Then have her use a brad to join the two patterns as shown. Just spin the wheel to see the fun friends can have—together!

5

ART SMARTS

Togetherness and friendship go hand in hand, as you can easily demonstrate with this good-friends garland. In advance, accordion-fold a 6" x 18" strip of white construction paper three times to make four sections. Trace a very simple person shape (as shown) on the folded paper; then cut along your outline, being careful not to cut the edges of the arms. Unfold the paper to reveal a string of four friends. Repeat this procedure until you have one paper friend for each child in your class. Place the strings of friends in your art center, along with a supply of crayons that include various skin tones.

Invite students to visit your art center in pairs. Have each child in the pair color a paper friend to resemble her real friend, carefully choosing crayons to match her friend's skin, hair, eyes, and clothing. When she's finished, have her model as her partner decorates a paper friend in *her* image. After every child has decorated a paper friend, use clear tape to attach the strings of four friends into one long chain. Display the chain on a bulletin board with the title "Hand in Hand, Friends Go Together."

PURPOSEFUL PLAY

The friends in *Together* show that it takes two to do many things! Bring home the importance of cooperation by providing some games that need to be played by more than one person. Set up a center with games such as Go Fish, Concentration, and tic-tac-toe. Invite pairs of children to visit this center to play—together, of course!

STORYBOOK CAFÉ

It takes a whole lot of togetherness to make this salad a success! In advance, send home a note to parents (similar to the one shown). Then get ready for some cooperative cooking!

Dear Family:
    We will be celebrating the true spirit of friendship by creating a Friendship Salad on _____. Please have your child bring a
(date)
piece of his or her favorite fruit to share that day.
    Thank you!

Friendship Salad

Supplies:
plastic knives
plastic spoons
disposable bowls
1 large bowl
1 large spoon

Ingredients:
fresh fruit provided by students

To make friendship salad:
1. Have each child wash and/or peel his piece of fruit.
2. Have each child use a plastic knife to cut his fruit into small slices or pieces.
3. Place all the cut fruit into a large bowl.
4. Scoop the fruit into individual bowls.

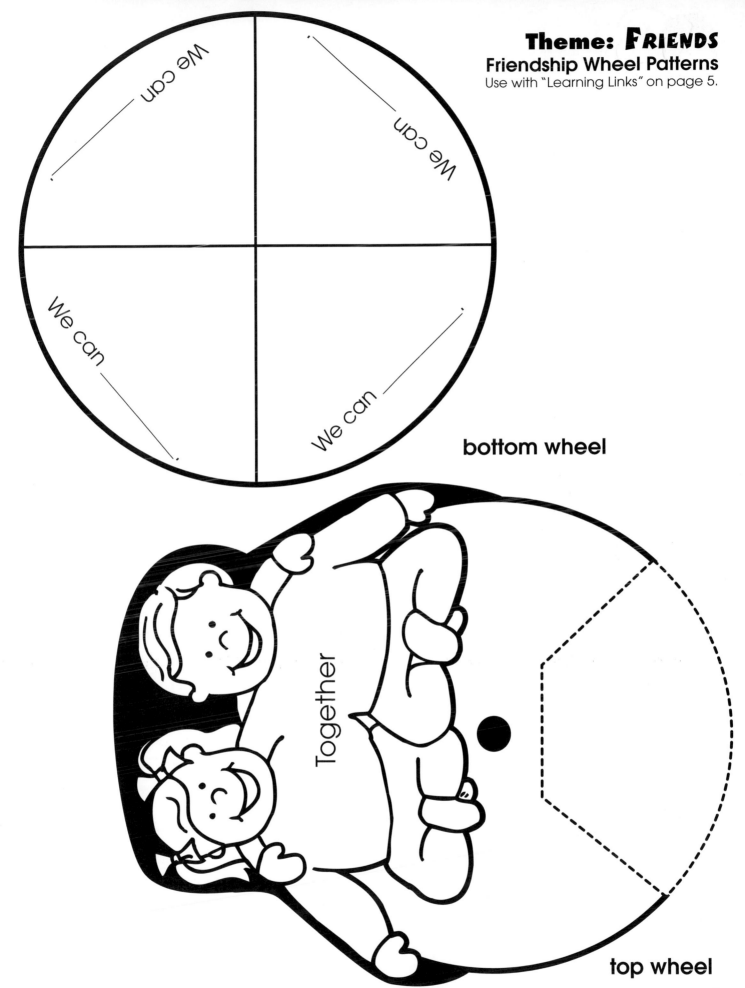

We can

We can

We can

We can

bottom wheel

Together

top wheel

WE ARE BEST FRIENDS

Written & Illustrated by Aliki

When your best friend moves away, life can seem so sad—until you meet a new friend who makes things not so bad!

 **READING CIRCLE**

Sing this song about friendship to the tune of "She'll Be Comin' Round the Mountain" to invite your youngsters to storytime.

> Join me for a story about friends.
> Join me for a story about friends.
> Oh, dear, what can you say
> When your best friend moves away?
> Oh, join me for this story about friends.

(Repeat until all your students have gathered in your reading circle.)

Once your little ones are ready to listen, read aloud *We Are Best Friends*.

 **LEARNING LINKS**

—Language Arts

Like Robert and Peter in Aliki's story, your little ones will enjoy writing to friends. Encourage youngsters to make some new friends by arranging for them to write to pen pals. Contact a teaching colleague at another school (either local or in another state) and exchange class lists. Have each student write or dictate a letter to a child from the other class. Encourage each youngster to include a photo of himself, brought from home. (If desired, use the stationery described in "Art Smarts" on page 9.) Mail the letters and wait for a response. If your pen pals are local, you may want to arrange a meeting after a few letters are exchanged.

For younger students, adapt this activity by writing a class letter on a large sheet of chart paper. Invite each child to contribute to the information you include by telling about your students and their interests. Add a class photo before folding and mailing the letter, addressed to your colleague's class.

Emily Johnson
Center School
Anytown, USA

Hi, Emily!
My name is
Carlos. I am 5.

ART SMARTS

Writing to a friend will be even more fun when little ones use this special stationery they create themselves! In advance, make a photocopy of each child's school photo. Then prepare some potato printers. To make one, slice off the end of a potato. Carve a simple shape, such as a heart or a circle, into this flat area; then cut away about a quarter inch of the potato around the shape, making it raised. Allow the potato printers to dry before using them.

For each child, glue the photocopy of her school photo near the top of a sheet of white copy paper. Have each youngster decorate her stationery by dipping a potato printer into a shallow container of tempera paint, then pressing it onto her paper near the edge. Have her continue with other potato printers and paint colors, creating a patterned border around her paper. Allow the paint to dry before making a few photo-copies. Slip the stationery into a large zippered plastic bag and attach an adhesive label that reads "The fun never ends when you're writing to a friend!" Have each child use her stationery when she writes to a pen pal (see "Learning Links" on page 8) or send the stationery home.

PURPOSEFUL PLAY

Being a good friend takes a lot of co-operation, as does this game of Friendship Tag. In a large open space, designate a circular boundary for the game. Choose one child to be It. Once It has tagged another child, that child links his arm through It's arm and they both work together to tag another child. Each time another child is tagged, he joins the chain of friends. When all the children are part of the chain, begin again with a new child as It.

STORYBOOK CAFÉ

Yum! These edible necklaces will make two friends *very* happy!

Best Friends Necklaces

Supplies:
1 paper circle (2" in diameter) per child
crayons
scissors
hole puncher

Ingredients:
Froot Loops® cereal
Gummi Savers® candy
licorice laces (2 per child)

To make one best friends necklace:
1. Copy the words "Best Friends" on the circle. Then cut it in half. Punch a hole in the top of each half.
2. Thread a licorice lace through the hole in one of the half circles.
3. Alternating five pieces of Froot Loops cereal and one Gummi Savers candy, lace the cereal and candy onto either side of the paper half circle until the necklace is complete.
4. Use the other half circle and the other licorice lace to make another necklace for a friend!
5. After you and your friend eat the cereal and candy, take the half circles off and put them back together to form the words "Best Friends."

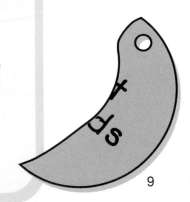

STELLALUNA

Written & Illustrated by Janell Cannon

"Flap" through the pages of this adventure, and you'll meet a little bat who learns that being friends doesn't always mean being alike.

  # READING CIRCLE

Call little ones to storytime with this enchanting song about Stellaluna, sung to the tune of "Are You Sleeping?"

> Stellaluna,
> Stellaluna,
> The friendly bat,
> The friendly bat.
> Come and hear her story
> In our reading circle,
> Friends, friends, friends,
> Friends, friends, friends.

(Repeat until all your little bats have flapped into your reading area.)

Once your youngsters are gathered in your group area, read aloud *Stellaluna*.

 # LEARNING LINKS

—Social Studies

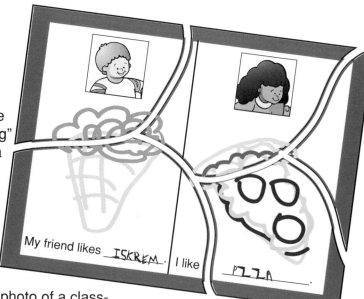

Like Stellaluna and her bird friends, friends can be very different. Explore this concept with this "puzzling" activity. In advance, draw a line down the center of a sheet of white copy paper and program it as shown. Photocopy the programmed sheet to make a class supply. Also photocopy a large supply of your students' school photos and cut them apart. Set these materials on a table, along with sheets of construction paper.

Have each child prepare a friendship puzzle. First, have her find a copy of her own photo and the photo of a classmate. Direct her to glue her classmate's photo to the top left side of her programmed sheet and her own photo to the top right. Then have her write or dictate an ending for each sentence and add illustrations. Have her glue her paper onto a larger sheet of construction paper. Laminate all the completed pictures; then cut each one into four or five large pieces. Place each child's puzzle in a separate zippered plastic bag. Send each

puzzle home to be reassembled and to spark a family discussion about friendship.

ART SMARTS

Friends will go batty over these sweet gifts! To prepare, use an X-acto® knife to cut a very simple bat shape from the center of a plastic lid. Then have each child paint a tree trunk on one side of a 12" x 18" sheet of white construction paper, adding a long branch that stretches across the page (as shown). When the paint is dry, have the child position the plastic lid (flat against the paper) so that the bat's head on the cutout is facing down and the bat's bottom is almost touching the branch. Direct her to use a sponge dipped in black paint to fill in the cutout. Have her lift the lid and repeat the process to create another bat. After the paint dries, have her draw legs for each bat so the bats appear to hang from the branch. Then have each child copy this text on her picture: "I like hanging out with you!" Invite each child to present her finished picture to a good friend.

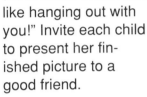

I like hanging out with you!

PURPOSEFUL PLAY

Here's a new twist on an old favorite—Duck, Duck, Goose. Gather your class into a circle. Select one child to be the bat. Have him walk around the outside of the circle, tapping each child on the head and saying "bird" until he decides to choose a new "bat." The new bat jumps up and flies (chases) after the original bat, trying to tag him. If he is tagged, the old bat climbs into the nest (the center of the circle), until a new bat is tagged. Now, *that's* a game to flap your wings about!

STORYBOOK CAFÉ

Grab a friend and work together to make these tasty treats!

Bat Bite Cupcakes

Supplies:
small paper plates
craft sticks

Ingredients:
1 unfrosted cupcake per child
chocolate frosting
M&Ms® candies
candy corn
chocolate-covered cookies (such as Keebler® Grasshoppers®), cut into quarters

To make one bat bite cupcake:
1. Use a craft stick to spread chocolate frosting onto a cupcake.
2. Add two M&M's candies for eyes.
3. Add two pieces of candy corn for fangs.
4. Add two cookie quarters for ears.

11

HOW TO LOSE ALL YOUR FRIENDS

Written & Illustrated by Nancy Carlson

Here are six rules friends never follow, but they're sure to have your little ones giggling!

READING CIRCLE

Youngsters will be intrigued about the subject of this silly book when you sing this musical invitation to the tune of "My Bonnie Lies Over the Ocean!"

You've heard how to have lots of friends.
You've heard all about being nice.
Well, this is where that lecture ends!
This book's full of *different* advice!
Let's read, let's read,
Let's read *How to Lose All Your Friends* today.
Let's read, let's read,
Let's read *How to Lose All Your Friends*!

(Repeat until all your little listeners have gathered in the reading circle.)

Once students are settled in for storytime, read aloud *How to Lose All Your Friends.*

LEARNING LINKS

—Language Arts

After reading all the rules for losing friends, it's time to create some rules for keeping friends! Brainstorm a list of rules for keeping friends, starting, of course, with the opposite of each rule given in Carlson's book. Record each rule on a blank sheet of paper. Then have students (or student pairs) illustrate the pages. Collect all the completed pages and form a class book. Add a cover with the title "How to Keep All Your Friends." This will make a handy reference guide for those times when someone forgets the importance of friendship.

ART SMARTS

This creative activity will help students appreciate the importance of having friends. To begin, have students pair up. Place a blindfold on one child in each pair, and provide him with a sheet of paper and a pencil. Show the remaining child in each pair a simple picture (such as a drawing of a cat). Have her provide directions for the blindfolded child on how to copy the picture, without actually telling her partner what the picture shows. For example, a child might say, "Draw a circle. Now draw two triangles on top…," etc. When the picture is complete, ask the artist to guess what he has drawn. Remove the blindfold and allow the children to enjoy a laugh! Then repeat the process, having the other child wear the blindfold and providing a different drawing to be copied.

PURPOSEFUL PLAY

Creative dramatics take on a whole new twist with this playful activity. In advance, record each of the instructions for losing your friends (from Carlson's book) on an individual index card. Select two children to act out each rule. Then ask them to try acting out a way to *keep* your friends instead. Then keep the activity going with a new pair of actors and a new rule.

STORYBOOK CAFÉ

As the story says, the number one rule for losing friends is to frown. Make these snacks as a friendly reminder to SMILE!

Pizza Smiles

(makes 16)

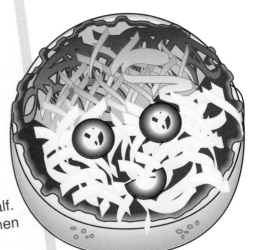

Ingredients:
8 English muffins (one half per child)
8-oz. can tomato sauce
2 cups shredded mozzarella cheese
1 cup shredded cheddar cheese
2¼-oz. can sliced black olives

Supplies:
plastic spoons
plastic knives
small paper plates
toaster oven

To make one pizza smile:
1. Spread two spoonfuls of tomato sauce onto an English muffin half.
2. Sprinkle shredded mozzarella cheese all over the muffin half. Then sprinkle shredded cheddar at the top to make hair.
3. Add two olive-slice eyes.
4. Cut one olive slice in half. Use one half to make a smile. Share the other half with a friend!
5. Bake in the toaster oven until the cheese is bubbly.

THE BABY SISTER

Written and Illustrated by Tomie dePaola

Tommy wants a baby sister with a red ribbon in her hair. Will he get one? And will he get along with his grandmother who comes to take care of him while his mother is in the hospital? Share Tommy's anticipation and excitement in this story about a new baby joining the family.

READING CIRCLE

Call your little listeners to your reading circle with this song sung to the tune of "A-Tisket A-Tasket."

A baby! A baby!
There's going to be a baby!
In this story Tommy wants
To have a little sister.
A sister, a sister,
Oh, will he get a sister?
Come to reading circle and
We'll all find out together!

(Repeat until all your students have gathered in the reading area.)

When everyone is settled in for storytime, read aloud *The Baby Sister.*

LEARNING LINKS

—Language Arts

When Tommy holds his baby sister at the end of the story, he is "the happiest boy in the world." Ask each student to think of a favorite time she has spent with a sibling (or a cousin or playmate if she is an only child). After inviting some youngsters to share their ideas, provide each child with a sheet of white drawing paper and crayons. Invite each of your little ones to draw herself and a sibling enjoying an activity or special time together. Then have her write or dictate about her drawing. Regroup and allow each child to share her picture. Then compile the completed pages into a class book with the title "Special Siblings."

I like to play hockey with my brother, Mike.

ART SMARTS

Tommy's wonderful pictures were a bright addition to the nursery. Brighten up the maternity ward of your local hospital by having students paint pictures for new mothers and babies to enjoy. In advance, contact the director of the maternity ward to be sure pictures will be accepted. Then provide students with art paper and watercolor paints. Invite each child to create a warm, happy picture for the new moms and babies. You might also have students dictate notes to the new moms. Deliver the packet of artwork and notes to the maternity ward, and be sure to include a return address, in case any new mothers wish to respond.

PURPOSEFUL PLAY

Caring for a newborn is a lot of work! Ask your students to brainstorm a list of the many responsibilities Tommy's family will have in caring for their new addition. Record the ideas on chart paper and add drawings to help nonreaders. Post the chart in your dramatic-play area; then stock the area to resemble a nursery, complete with baby dolls, blankets, doll diapers, baby toys, bottles, and any other baby equipment you can gather. Invite children to visit the area in pairs, as they imitate family members caring for a new baby.

STORYBOOK CAFÉ

Encourage each student to create this baby sister snack—complete with a red bow!

Sister Snacks

Supplies:
craft sticks
paper plates

Ingredients for each child:
1 large round cracker
2 triangle crackers
1 Ritz® Bits® sandwich
soft cream cheese
raisins
strawberry jam

To make one sister snack:
1. Spread cream cheese on the round cracker.
2. Add raisin eyes and a raisin mouth.
3. Spread strawberry jam on the two triangle crackers and on the Ritz Bits sandwich.
4. Arrange the jam-covered crackers to form a bow above the face (as shown).

I CAN! CAN YOU?

Written by Carol Adorjan
Illustrated by Miriam Nerlove

Older sisters can do so much—but so can little sisters! Share this inspiring look at the flourishing independence of younger siblings.

READING CIRCLE

Encourage young readers to join you for a story with this song sung to the tune of "I'm a Little Teapot."

Come read about a sister, short and smart.
She uses her brain; she uses her heart!
We're sure to see her try and try again.
Come to the circle as I count to ten.
1, 2, 3, 4, 5, 6, 7, 8, 9, 10

(Sing the verse; then slowly count to ten as youngsters make their way to the reading area.)

When you can see that your youngsters are ready to listen, read aloud *I Can! Can You?*

 **LEARNING LINKS**

—Language Arts

After sharing the story, ask your little ones to consider what tasks they are able to do. Have kindergarten students pair up; then ask them to interview one another to find out what each child can do. Have each child complete a copy of page 18 by drawing a picture of her buddy performing a task he is proud to be able to do. Help her fill in the blanks to describe the action. Try pairing younger children with older elementary buddies to help them complete this activity.

Invite students to share their completed pages before putting them on display in your classroom. What a wonderful way to boost self-esteem!

Someone I know can **ride a pony.**

That person is named **Maria**

ART SMARTS

Showcase your students' abilities by creating an "I Can!" quilt. Ask each student to think of a new accomplishment from the last few months. Provide each student with a 5" x 5" square of white copy paper and a 6" x 6" square of construction paper. Direct him to draw a picture showing his accomplishment on the white square, and to write or dictate a sentence telling about it. Then have him glue his white paper in the center of his colored paper. Assemble all the squares on a large rectangle of bulletin board paper to form a quilt, adding additional colored squares if necessary. Print the words "I Can!" on any additional squares or on the quilt border. Then display the "I Can!" quilt in a prominent area of your classroom.

PURPOSEFUL PLAY

Your youngsters will be showing off their many talents in this adaptation of Follow the Leader. To begin, gather students in a circle. Say, "I can touch my toes. Can you?" Encourage students to mimic you as you touch your toes. Then invite the child beside you to name an action and model it for everyone else to copy. Remind her to ask, "Can you?" Bet they can!

STORYBOOK CAFÉ

Small groups of youngsters *can* help make this yummy frozen treat, and then they *can* eat it!

I Can! Ice Cream
(makes 6 servings)

Supplies:
large mixing bowl
hand mixer
rubber spatula
measuring cups
6 small metal juice cans (1 per child)
plastic spoons

Ingredients:
2 cups whipping cream
2/3 cup sweetened condensed milk
2/3 cup chocolate syrup
1/3 cup mini chocolate chips (optional)

To make I can! ice cream:
1. Combine cream, milk, and syrup in the mixing bowl. Beat with the hand mixer until stiff peaks form.
2. Fold in mini chocolate chips (if desired).
3. Divide the mixture evenly among the 6 juice cans.
4. Freeze until firm.

17

Someone I know can _____

_____.

That person is named _____.

SHEILA RAE, THE BRAVE

Written and Illustrated by Kevin Henkes

Sheila Rae is a fearless mouse who looks out for her little sister, Louise. But it's Louise who comes to the rescue when Sheila Rae takes her fearlessness too far.

READING CIRCLE

Invite students to your reading circle with this song sung to the tune of "Five Little Ducks."

> One little mouse,
> Named Sheila Rae,
> She was brave, both night and day!
> Sheila Rae, she had no fear,
> Till she got lost—oh, dear! Oh, dear!
>
> Come and read
> This story now.
> A sister helped—you'll find out how.
> In this story we will hear
> Of Sheila Rae, who has no fear!

(Repeat the verses until all your little mice have gathered for storytime.)

When youngsters are seated, read aloud *Sheila Rae, the Brave.*

 ## LEARNING LINKS

—Critical Thinking

Although Sheila Rae was a brave little mouse, she also made some unsafe choices. After sharing the story, provide a copy of page 21 for each student. Direct each child to color and cut out the pictures along the bottom edge. Have him determine whether each action is safe or unsafe and glue the picture in the appropriate column. Ask each student to use the back of his paper to draw a picture of Sheila Rae and Louise doing something brave *and safe* together.

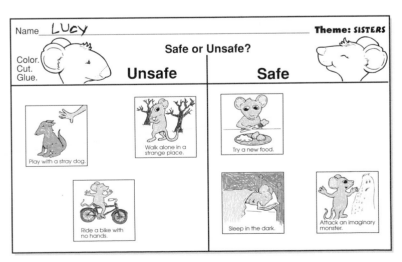

—Character Building

Your youngsters are sure to feel more courageous when they're wearing these Bravery Badges. Provide each child with a small paper plate labeled as shown. Ask her to draw herself doing something brave or difficult, such as jumping off the diving board at the pool or eating a new food. Punch a hole at the top of each completed badge; then thread it onto an 18-inch length of ribbon. Tie the ribbon loosely around the brave badge maker's neck. Invite little ones to wear their badges to boost their bravery throughout the day.

Bravery Badge

ART SMARTS

Be brave! Invite your little ones to try their hands at making these sock mice. Direct each child to stuff a white baby sock with cotton balls or polyester fiber-fill to within about two inches of the cuff. Twist a white pipe cleaner around the opening to close it; then have the child wrap the free end of the pipe cleaner around and around the remaining cuff, leaving the loose end of the pipe cleaner to form the tail. Provide each child with a small piece of white or pink felt and have her cut out two round ears. Help her glue the ears in place using fabric glue. Have her add two small wiggle eyes and use a black marker to draw a nose and whiskers. If desired, reread the story and invite youngsters to act out Sheila's part with their completed mice.

STORYBOOK CAFÉ

These yummy treats are perfect for little mice—they're cheesy and they're easy!

Cheesecake Delights
(makes 24)

Supplies:
large mixing bowl
hand mixer
large spoon
measuring cups and spoons
foil baking cups
muffin tins
plastic spoons

Ingredients:
four 8-oz. packages cream
 cheese, softened
4 eggs
1 cup sugar
4 tsp. vanilla
24 vanilla wafers
21-oz. can cherry, blueberry,
 or strawberry pie filling

To make cheesecake delights:
1. Combine cream cheese, eggs, sugar, and vanilla. Beat with hand mixer for five minutes or until smooth.
2. Place baking cups in muffin tins.
3. Place a vanilla wafer in the bottom of each cup.
4. Divide cheesecake mixture evenly between cups.
5. Bake at 375° for 15 minutes.
6. Cool. Top each snack with a spoonful of pie filling.

Name _____

Safe or Unsafe?

Color.
Cut.
Glue.

Unsafe | **Safe**

Walk alone in a strange place.

Attack an imaginary monster.

Ride a bike with no hands.

Try a new food.

Sleep in the dark.

Play with a stray dog.

©2000 The Education Center, Inc. • *Booktime!* • *People* • TEC1704

21

SHE COME BRINGING ME THAT LITTLE BABY GIRL

Written by Eloise Greenfield
Illustrated by John Steptoe

Kevin is eager for his mother to bring home a baby boy from the hospital. But she brings him a girl instead. It is only when he understands the importance of being a big brother that he embraces his new sister.

READING CIRCLE

Send youngsters a musical invitation to the reading circle with this song sung to the tune of "Mary Had a Little Lamb."

Come and meet a little boy,
Little boy, little boy.
Come and meet a little boy
Who wants a baby brother.
Mom brings home a little girl,
Little girl, little girl.
Mom brings home a little girl—
And now he wants no other!

(Repeat the verse until all your students have gathered in your reading area.)

When your little ones are ready, read aloud *She Come Bringing Me That Little Baby Girl.*

LEARNING LINKS

—Language Arts

When you read the book aloud, pause after sharing the cover, title page, and first page of text. Ask students to predict how Kevin might be feeling about "that little baby girl." Then read the rest of the story. Discuss how Kevin's feelings changed and why. Then ask youngsters to think of some experiences when they felt sad or angry and how their feelings changed. Provide each child with a sheet of white drawing paper cut into a simple head-and-shoulders shape (as shown). Ask each child to draw a picture of herself feeling sad or angry on her cutout. Have her dictate a sentence or two telling when she felt this way. Then have her flip her cutout over and draw herself with a happy face. Have her dictate how and why her feelings changed. Punch a hole in the top of each child's cutout; then thread a length of yarn through theme hole and tie it in place. Display these two-sided pictures from your classroom ceiling.

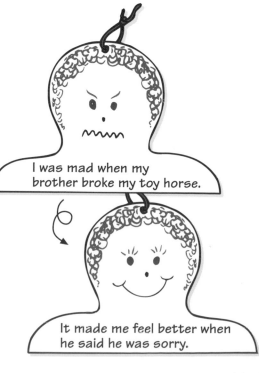

I was mad when my brother broke my toy horse.

It made me feel better when he said he was sorry.

—Math

Kevin was an only child until his little sister came along. How many children are in each of your students' families? Find out with this graph—the materials you'll need to make it are right at your fingertips! To prepare, cut a large piece of bulletin board paper and label it as shown. Then give each child a 4" x 4" square of light-colored construction paper, access to a variety of ink pads, and some thin markers. Direct each child to make one thumbprint on his square for each child in his family. Have him use the markers to add faces and clothing details as he desires. Have him glue the finished square to the graph in the appropriate row. When the graph is complete, encourage students to share their observations. Discuss the results of the graph, emphasizing the concepts of *more, fewer,* and *equal.*

How many children are in your family?

1	□ □ □ □
2	□ □ □ □ □ □ □ □
3	□ □ □
4	□ □
5	
6	
7	□

STORYBOOK CAFÉ

These crunchy treats are sweet—just like most baby sisters!

Gingerbread Sisters
(makes approximately 20 large cookies)

Supplies:
large mixing bowl
large spoon
measuring cups and spoons
rolling pin
people-shaped cookie cutters
cookie sheets
plastic knives or craft sticks

Ingredients:
5 cups flour
$1\frac{1}{2}$ tsp. baking soda
2 tsp. ginger
1 tsp. cinnamon
$\frac{1}{2}$ tsp. salt
1 cup shortening
1 egg
$\frac{3}{4}$ cup molasses
$\frac{3}{4}$ cup honey
flour
frosting and tubes of decorator icing
decorating goodies (raisins, mini
    chocolate chips, sprinkles, etc.)

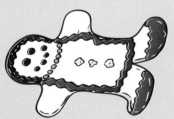

To make gingerbread sisters:
1. Mix together flour, baking soda, ginger, cinnamon, and salt.
2. Add shortening, egg, molasses, and honey. Mix well.
3. Roll the dough to $\frac{1}{4}$-inch thickness on a floured surface.
4. Cut out shapes with cutters. Place on cookie sheets.
5. Bake at 375° for 10 minutes.
6. When the cookies have cooled, frost and decorate as desired.

ART SMARTS

Kevin finally realized that being a big brother is an important job! Invite youngsters to explore their family roles with this art idea. In advance, duplicate the patterns on page 24 onto white construction paper. Working with one small group at a time, direct each student to cut out the patterns and assemble the head, shirt, and pants to create a person shape. Once she has glued these pieces together, invite her to color the clothing and make the face resemble her own. Provide several colors of yarn or paper scraps for creating hair. Then have her dictate a sentence or two about her role in her family as you write on the speech bubble. Make a prominent display of these very special paper people with their corresponding speech bubbles.

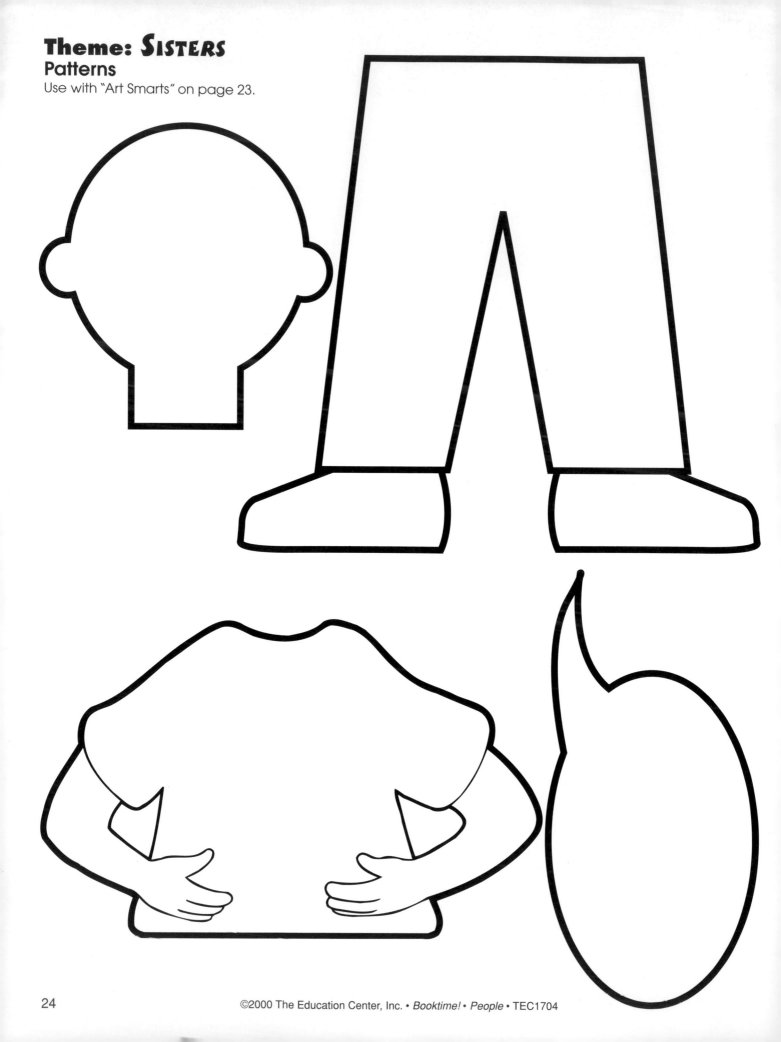

WHAT'S SO TERRIBLE ABOUT SWALLOWING AN APPLE SEED?

Written by Harriet Lerner and Susan Goldhor
Illustrated by Catharine O'Neill

When little Rosie swallows an apple seed, her big sister Katie convinces her that it will grow into an apple tree in her tummy. Playful illustrations give life to this delightful story about sisterhood and the power of imagination.

READING CIRCLE

Call students to storytime by singing these lines to the tune of "There Was an Old Lady Who Swallowed a Fly."

There was a young girl who swallowed a seed.
I don't know why she swallowed a seed.
Oh, my! Indeed!
Her sister told her she'd grow a tree,
Grow a tree right out of that seed.
Oh, my! Indeed!
Please join me now so I can read
About the girl who swallowed a seed.
Oh, my! Indeed!

(Repeat the verse until all your little ones have come to the reading circle.)

Once your group is settled, read aloud *What's So Terrible About Swallowing an Apple Seed?*

 ## LEARNING LINKS

—Science

Expand on Katie's bedtime story by having children create this four-seasons chart. Ask students to recall the seasonal events that happened to the girl with the apple tree branches in the bedtime story. Then have students brainstorm other ideas for each season. Record their ideas on a sheet of chart paper divided into four columns. Then divide the class into four groups. Assign each group a season and provide them with a 12" x 18" sheet of white construction paper. Ask the members of each group to help illustrate the ideas for its season. Display the completed artwork with the chart in your writing center to inspire your young storytellers.

Spring	Summer	Fall	Winter
smells good	makes cool shade	make applesauce	make nests for birds
birds singing on branches	don't need umbrella if it rains	class field trip to pick apples	hang bird feeders on branches
make flower bouquets			decorate branches with lights

ART SMARTS

—Language Arts

Use this story to jump-start a lesson about fiction and nonfiction. To prepare, cut a large apple shape from red bulletin board paper and label it "Apple Facts." First, explain to little ones the difference between *fiction* (made-up stories) and *nonfiction* (facts and information). Then share a variety of books about apples, including some stories and some informational books. After reading each book, ask students to tell you whether it was fiction or nonfiction. From each nonfiction book, ask them to recall some facts about apples to record on your chart. Then help youngsters put their newfound apple knowledge to work as they plant apple seeds. Provide cups, spoons, soil, apple seeds, and a watering can full of water. Invite each child to plant some apple seeds and observe their growth. After a few days, send the cups home and encourage little ones to share their knowledge about apples with their families as they continue to nurture their future apple trees!

These portraits of Rosie with her imagined apple tree growing out of her ears are an unforgettable art project! To begin, have each child decorate a thin white paper plate to resemble Rosie's face. Then have each child take a turn at your easel. Have her glue her paper-plate face to the bottom center of her sheet of easel paper. Then encourage her to paint the branches and leaves of an apple tree as if they originated in Rosie's ears, making them as long and luxurious as she likes! If desired, have her use a circle-shaped sponge to paint either pink blossoms or red apples on the tree branches.

STORYBOOK CAFÉ

If Rosie's seed *did* grow into an apple tree full of yummy apples, she'd surely want this dip to go with them!

Apple Dips
(serves 24)

Supplies:
large mixing bowl
large spoon
paper plates
sharp knife or apple cutter
  (for teacher's use)

Ingredients:
two 8-oz. packages cream
  cheese, softened
2 jars marshmallow creme
3 red apples, cut into 8 pieces
3 green apples, cut into 8 pieces
3 yellow apples, cut into 8 pieces

To make apple dips:
1. Mix together cream cheese and marshmallow creme.
2. Serve a large spoonful of dip with one slice of each color apple.

HARRY AND TUCK

Written and Illustrated by Holly Keller

Harry and Tuck have always done everything together. What will happen on the first day of kindergarten when they discover that they are not in the same class?

READING CIRCLE

Call your students to the reading circle with this verse set to the tune of "Jack and Jill."

> Harry and Tuck went off to school,
> A-walkin' with each other.
> Each went to his own classroom,
> But how he missed his brother!

(Repeat the verse until all your little ones have gathered in the reading circle.)

Once students have come a-walkin' to your reading circle, read aloud *Harry and Tuck.*

 ## LEARNING LINKS

—Basic Concepts

Examine with your students the book pages on which Harry and Tuck are dressed alike. Point out that the boys are a matching pair in each illustration. Then challenge youngsters to brainstorm items that come in matching pairs, such as shoes, socks, or gloves. Remind them that they also have body-part pairs, such as hands, feet, ears, and knees. Then follow up with a matching activity.

Pair students; then ask each child to trace around her partner's hands or shoes. Have each child decorate her outlines to make a matching pair. Then have her cut them out and label the back of each one with her name. Place all the hand cutouts in one basket and all the shoe cutouts in another. Place the baskets in a center for visual skills practice. Invite a child or a pair of children to spread out all the cutouts from one basket on a table (faceup). Have the players find all the matching pairs. They can check their work by looking at the names on the backs of the cutouts.

27

ART SMARTS

In the story, both Harry and Tuck like the color green. Celebrate this special color by making green collages. Stock your art center with an assortment of green items, such as stickers, sequins, ribbon, fabric squares, glitter, cellophane scraps, Easter grass, paper scraps, leaves, and dyed pasta or rice. Also provide green paint, markers, crayons, glue, and stamp pads. Then give each visitor a sheet of green construction paper. Encourage him to use the green items to create a collage. Display these masterpieces with the title "Green Is Great!"

PURPOSEFUL PLAY

This fun game will hold youngsters' attention as well as demonstrate how Harry and Tuck did everything together. To begin, divide your class into student pairs and designate one child in each pair as the leader for the first round of play. Have each child stand facing her partner as if looking into a mirror. Then call out a body part, such as hand, head, mouth, or leg. On a signal, the leader in each pair will slowly move the named body part. Her partner should mimic her movement to create a mirror image. The pair continues moving until you give a signal to stop. Then have the partners switch roles for the next round of play.

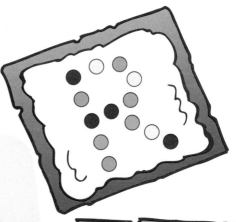

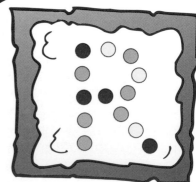

STORYBOOK CAFÉ

Double your students' snack pleasure with these special goodies.

Twin Treats

Supplies:
napkins
plastic knives

Ingredients:
2 graham cracker halves per child
marshmallow creme
M&M's® brand mini baking bits

To make twin treats:
1. Spread marshmallow creme on each cracker half.
2. Arrange baking bits in a pattern or design on one cracker.
3. Repeat the same pattern or design on the second cracker.

I LOVE YOU THE PURPLEST

Written by Barbara M. Joosse
Illustrated by Mary Whyte

"Who do you love best?" each of two brothers secretly asks Mama after a day of competing for her attention. Mama's gentle response is unique to each boy and conveys the strong, unconditional nature of a parent's love.

READING CIRCLE

Encourage young readers to join you for storytime by singing this song to the tune of "The Muffin Man."

> Come hear a story of two young boys,
> Two young boys, two young boys.
> Come hear a story of two young boys
> Whose mama loves them so!
>
> Yes, Mama loves each of her boys,
> Each of her boys, each of her boys.
> Yes, Mama loves each of her boys,
> In a very special way!

(Repeat until all the children have joined the circle.)

Once all your students are settled in for a story, read aloud *I Love You the Purplest.*

LEARNING LINKS

—Math

Max, Julian, and Mama enjoy a moonlight fishing trip, and your little ones will enjoy a trip to your math center to play this fishing game. To prepare, make a supply of fish by photocopying the patterns on page 31 onto construction paper. Cut out each fish; then program it with a dot set or a numeral from 1 to 10. Attach a metal paper clip to each fish and then put all the fish in a large plastic tub. Arrange the tub, a magnetic fishing pole, and a container of fish-shaped crackers in your math center. Invite each child who visits this center to use the fishing pole to catch a paper fish. Have him count the dots (or identify the numeral) and then take a matching number of crackers as his fisherman's meal. Or—for more of a challenge—have him catch two fish and compare them to determine which fish shows the greater quantity (or number). Then invite him to count out that many crackers to eat.

ART SMARTS

Mama loves Julian the bluest and Max the reddest. And when she blends her love for her two boys, she loves them both together the purplest. Invite youngsters to blend some red and blue paint to create these purple hearts. At your art center, provide each child with a small Styrofoam® cup containing some red and blue tempera paint. Have her use a paintbrush to thoroughly mix the two colors together. Then invite her to add small amounts of either color until she achieves a shade of purple she likes. Next have her paint a large heart on a sheet of white paper. When the paint dries, have her cut out the heart and dictate a love message for you to write on the back. Encourage each child to deliver the special heart to the person she loves the purplest.

Daddy,
I love you
when you read
to me.
John

Blue   Red

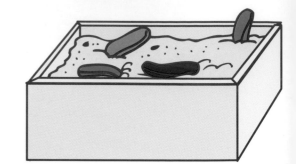

PURPOSEFUL PLAY

Dig into this sand table activity to reinforce color recognition and sorting skills. To begin, cut a supply of worm shapes from various craft foam colors. Then label a separate canister for each worm color. Bury the foam worms in your sand table. Add some sand scoops and rakes to the table; then place the labeled canisters nearby. Invite youngsters who visit this center to dig up the worms, sort them into the canisters by color, and then count how many of each they've found.

As a variation, cut both short and long worms from the foam and encourage students to sort the worms by color *and* length.

STORYBOOK CAFÉ

Youngsters will agree that this lake filled with fishes is really delicious!

Rice Cake Lake

Supplies:
small paper plates
plastic knives or craft sticks

Ingredients:
1 rice cake per child
soft cream cheese, tinted blue
fish-shaped crackers

To make one rice cake lake:
1. Spread blue cream cheese on the rice cake.
2. Put several fish crackers in the cream cheese "water."

TIDY TITCH

Written and Illustrated by Pat Hutchins

Titch's room is very tidy—until he helps his siblings clean their rooms!

READING CIRCLE

Hold up the book so youngsters can see its cover and invite them to join you in the reading circle. Sing this song to the tune of "Twinkle, Twinkle, Little Star" as they're making their way over.

> When brother and sister cleaned their rooms,
> They gave Titch some cars that zoom,
> A big dollhouse, a cool space suit,
> A bear and monkey—soft and cute.
> Now their rooms are clean and right,
> But Titch's room is quite a sight!

(Repeat until your little ones have gathered for storytime.)

When your students are all in their places, read aloud *Tidy Titch.*

LEARNING LINKS

—Science

Cleaning a room calls for sorting and categorizing skills. Help little ones use those same skills in this activity that may help with your classroom management as well! To prepare, gather a collection of classroom items and toys that belong to different categories, such as stuffed animals, vehicles, blocks, and scissors. Put all the items in a large box. Then label a separate container for each category. Working with one small group at a time, have a student select an item from the large box and place it in the appropriately labeled container. Repeat this procedure until all the items are sorted. Then ask youngsters to point out the proper classroom location for each set of items. Remind youngsters to always return classroom materials to their appropriate places after work or play.

ART SMARTS

Encourage youngsters to put toys in their proper place with these personalized toy boxes. For each child, cut a hinged door from a sheet of construction paper (as shown). To create a toy box, glue the construction paper door onto another sheet of construction paper so that the door—or lid—is left free to open and close. Personalize each child's toy box; then invite the child to decorate it with a variety of art materials. Afterward, have her cut out small pictures of favorite toys from toy catalogs, sales flyers, or family magazines. Have her lift the lid of her toy box and glue the pictures inside. During a group time, encourage each child to share the contents of her box with classmates.

Emma's Toy Box

STORYBOOK CAFÉ

This neat treat will make a yummy snack for your tidy snackers.

Supplies:
napkins
plastic knives

Tidy Tidbits

Ingredients for each child:
8 Cheese Nips® crackers
soft cheese spread (such as pimento cheese or cream cheese)
4 olive slices or small cucumber chunks

To make tidy tidbits:
1. Spread the soft cheese on one cracker.
2. Add another cracker on top of the spread.
3. Top the stack with an olive slice or cucumber chunk.
4. Repeat to make three more tidy tidbits.

PURPOSEFUL PLAY

All of your students will turn into tidy Titches when they play this fun relay! To prepare, gather one wooden or foam block per child. (If your class is small, you may want to use two blocks per child.) Divide the quantity of blocks in half; then pile each set at one end of an open classroom area. Place a sheet of paper next to each pile. Divide your class into two teams and have each team line up, one child behind another, directly across the open area from one of the block piles. To play, the first child in each line runs to his team's block pile, removes a block, and places it on the paper. Then he runs back to his line and tags the next player. That child runs to the pile, removes a second block, and neatly stacks it atop the first. She then runs back to her team and tags a third player. Play continues until one team has had all its members contribute to creating a neat and tidy block tower. If a tower falls over during play, the team must rebuild it.

For more of a challenge, provide each team with two block colors and ask them to build a tower with an alternating color pattern.

SHE COME BRINGING ME THAT LITTLE BABY GIRL

Written by Eloise Greenfield
Illustrated by John Steptoe

Kevin wants a brother, but Mama brings a baby girl home from the hospital instead. With sensitivity and understanding, Mama helps convert his disappointment into big-brother pride.

READING CIRCLE

Invite young readers to listen to this story by singing this song to the tune of "She'll Be Coming Round the Mountain."

> Oh, what is Mama bringing home today?
> Oh, what is Mama bringing home today?
> Will it be a baby brother?
> Will it be a baby sister?
> Come find out at our storytime today!

(Repeat until all the children have gathered in your reading circle.)

Once youngsters are ready, read aloud *She Come Bringing Me That Little Baby Girl.*

LEARNING LINKS

—Language Arts

Do any of your youngsters have babies in their families? If so, invite them to share their experiences and tell about being an older sibling. After discussing the pros and cons of living with a new baby, give each child a white construction paper copy of page 36. Have each child cut out the pattern and color the baby's blanket. Invite her to add a decorative bow or ribbon, if desired. Have each child use craft materials—such as wiggle eyes, yarn, and paint pens—to add a face to her baby. Then have her dictate a description of her baby on either a blue or a pink sentence strip to match the baby's gender. Invite each child to share her baby craft and description at a group time. Then display the projects with the title "Baby Brothers, Baby Sisters." Add the sentence strips as a border to entice admirers to match each baby to its description.

My baby has short hair.   She has a green blanket.

ART SMARTS

Use this fingerpainting technique—reminiscent of John Steptoe's illustrations—to reinforce youngsters' shape recognition and drawing skills. To begin, ask students to examine the layered outlines in the book's illustrations. Then invite them to create similar pictures with simple shapes. First, have a child fingerpaint a large solid shape in the center of a sheet of fingerpaint paper. Then have him outline the shape with a different color of paint. Have him continue to add outlines, each time a different color, until the page is full. After the paint dries, encourage each youngster to cut out his shape. These projects will make a colorful and shapely display!

PURPOSEFUL PLAY

In the story, Kevin knew just what he wanted to teach his little sister: how to throw a football! Use this circle game to boost self-esteem as youngsters express their special abilities. To begin, seat youngsters in a circle with their backs to the center. Designate one child as the parent. Give the parent a baby doll wrapped in a blanket. To play, the parent walks around the circle as you play a lullaby tape. When you stop the music, the parent carefully places the baby in the arms of the nearest child. That child—the older sibling—names something he can do that he'd like to teach the baby how to do, such as ride a bike or hop on one foot. Then the parent and sibling switch roles. Continue play until every child has had a turn to be both parent and sibling.

STORYBOOK CAFÉ

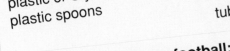

These footballs will be tasty reminders of Kevin's pride in being a big brother.

Fabulous Footballs

Ingredients for each child:
2 tbsp. peanut butter
1 tbsp. powdered milk
¼ cup crushed Cocoa Krispies® cereal
tube of decorator icing

Supplies:
waxed paper
plastic or Styrofoam® bowls
plastic spoons

To make one fabulous football:
1. Mix peanut butter and powdered milk in a bowl.
2. Stir in cereal.
3. Shape mixture into a football shape on waxed paper.
4. Use icing to make rings and stitching.

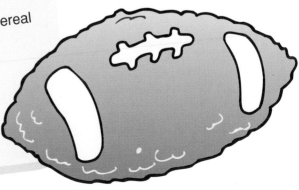

Theme: BROTHERS

Baby Pattern

Use with "Learning Links" on page 34.

Slither McCreep and His Brother, Joe

Written by Tony Johnston
Illustrated by Victoria Chess

What's a young snake to do when his brother won't share his toys? Slither's solution is to put the squeeze on Joe's toys. But when the broken toys and Joe's hurt feelings make Slither feel bad, he gets an idea that makes everyone happy!

Reading Circle

Invite students to gather in your reading circle by singing this song to the tune of "Three Blind Mice."

> Come, let's read,
> Come, let's read,
> About Slither McCreep
> And his brother, Joe.
> They're two little snakes who got into a fight.
> Slither got mad and he didn't act right.
> Is that the end? Oh, no—not quite!
> Come, let's read.
> Come, let's read.

(Repeat until all your little ones have slithered over to your reading circle.)

Once all your students have gathered in your circle area, read aloud *Slither McCreep and His Brother, Joe.*

Learning Links

—Math

Use a snake puppet to reinforce shape skills with your students. To make one, hot-glue wiggle eyes and a felt tongue onto the toe end of a kneesock. If desired, decorate the puppet with fabric paints. Then gather a variety of items in different shapes, such as small balls, wooden blocks, and cookie cutters. Slide several items into the snake puppet, leaving space between each one. Ask a child to look at and feel the shapes as she tries to identify each one. To further challenge students, gather identical pairs of objects. Place up to four different shapes inside the puppet, and leave the matching items visible on the tabletop. Have a child sequence the visible items to match the order of the shapes inside the snake puppet. What a s-s-super shapes skills workout!

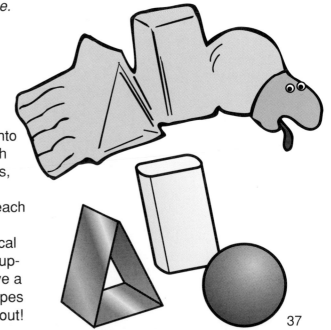

ART SMARTS

Squeeze some color skills into this play dough activity. Use purchased white play dough or prepare a batch using the recipe shown. Give each child a portion of dough and a small amount of fingerpaint in the color of his choice. Instruct him to squeeze the paint into the play dough to tint it. Then invite him to shape his play dough into different forms, such as snakes, balls, or geometric shapes.

Play Dough

1 cup flour
$\frac{1}{2}$ cup salt
2 tsp. cream of tartar
1 cup water
1 tsp. vegetable oil

Mix ingredients together in a saucepan. Heat the mixture, stirring constantly, until the desired consistency is achieved. Allow the play dough to cool before use.

STORYBOOK CAFÉ

This soft snake snack is s-s-simply s-s-super!

Snake Rollups

Supplies:
napkins
plastic knives

Ingredients for each child:
$\frac{1}{2}$ soft tortilla
cream cheese spread
2 shelled sunflower seeds
1 red pepper strip
spray cheese

To make one snake rollup:
1. Spread cream cheese on tortilla half.
2. Roll tortilla half toward straight edge.
3. Spread a small amount of cream cheese onto one end of the rolled tortilla.
4. Add sunflower-seed eyes and a red-pepper-strip tongue.
5. Decorate the snake's back with spray cheese.

PURPOSEFUL PLAY

How might a young snake play with a ball? Have youngsters examine the illustrations in the book, and they'll probably decide that it would use its tail! Invite a small or large group of students to play a game of Snake Ball. To prepare, cut a supply of one-inch loops from old hosiery. Arrange the desired number of chairs in a circle. Appoint one child to be the helper; then give him a playground ball. Have the other children—the snakes—sit in the chairs. Slip a hosiery loop around both ankles of each snake so that his legs must move as one (like a tail). To play, the helper rolls the ball into the circle. When the ball rolls within his reach, a snake kicks the ball to another snake, trying to keep the ball within the circle. Have the snakes count aloud the number of times the ball is kicked before it rolls out of the circle. Then have the helper retrieve it and roll it back into the circle for more play.

TELL ME AGAIN ABOUT THE NIGHT I WAS BORN

Written by Jamie Lee Curtis
Illustrated by Laura Cornell

Celebrate the birth of a family with this charming story. The vibrant watercolor illustrations burst with love between a child and her parents.

READING CIRCLE

Invite little ones to join the reading circle with this song sung to the tune of "Happy Birthday to You."

> Come to reading circle,
> Come to reading circle,
> Come to reading circle,
> And meet a new friend.
>
> Come hear the story,
> Come hear the story,
> Come hear the story
> Of the night she was born.

(Repeat the verses until all your youngsters have joined the circle.)

When everyone is ready for reading, share *Tell Me Again About the Night I Was Born*.

LEARNING LINKS

—Science

What stories have your students heard about the days they were born? Have your little ones seen pictures of themselves as newborns? Revisit the double-page illustration of the new baby. What do youngsters notice? After discussing the baby's features, provide each child with a 12" x 24" piece of butcher paper. Invite him to draw a life-size picture of himself as a new baby. Then supply watercolors so he can paint his picture just as Laura Cornell did the book's illustrations. Provide a black marker for each child to use to label his picture with his name; then add his birthdate. Display these very special baby pictures for your whole classroom family to admire!

ART SMARTS

The child in the story enjoys her parents' memories about the day she was born. What memories do your students treasure? Invite them to make "All About Me" boxes for storing their favorite mementos. Ask parents to send in shoeboxes, and be sure to have a few extras on hand for children who forget theirs. Encourage each child to paint her box, including the lid. When the paint is dry, have her personalize the lid (as shown) with a thick black marker. Later, when children aren't around, use a spray varnish on the boxes to give them a shiny finish. Then send the boxes home and invite youngsters to gather some favorite objects that spark happy memories. If desired, invite little ones to bring their boxes back to school to share the contents with classmates.

PURPOSEFUL PLAY

After little ones have thought about what they were like as babies, have them consider how much they have changed. Then encourage each child to make a life-size portrait of herself in her current size! Have each child lie faceup on a length of bulletin board paper as you trace around her body. Then have her use crayons to add features and clothing. Have a mirror or two nearby so little ones can get the details just right! Hang the finished body pictures next to the baby paintings and add the title "My, How We've Grown!"

STORYBOOK CAFÉ

The best thing about this clay is that children can play with it and eat it, too! Encourage them to use their clay to form the letters in their names.

Candy Clay
(makes 16 portions)

Supplies:
large bowl
mixing spoon
paper plates or waxed paper squares
$^1/_3$-cup measuring cup
teaspoon

Ingredients:
$^1/_3$ cup margarine
(at room temperature)
$^1/_3$ cup light corn syrup
1 tsp. vanilla or peppermint extract
1 box powdered sugar

To make candy clay:
1. Blend the margarine and corn syrup in a large bowl.
2. Stir in flavoring.
3. Mix in two-thirds of the box of powdered sugar with the spoon.
4. Add the last of the powdered sugar; then knead with your hands until all the sugar is mixed in and the dough is smooth.
5. Divide the dough into 16 portions.
6. Have each child work with a portion on a paper plate or square of waxed paper.

JUST LIKE MY DAD

Written by Tricia Gardella
Illustrated by Margot Apple

Saddle your ponies and ride along with a little cowpoke and his dad as they go about their daily routine on the ranch—mending fences, herding cattle, and listening to the old-timers' tales.

READING CIRCLE

Round up your little cowpokes and head for the reading circle as you sing these verses to the tune of "Pawpaw Patch."

One little, two little, three little cowpokes,
Four little, five little, six little cowpokes,
Seven little, eight little, nine little cowpokes,
Ten little cowpokes on roundup day!

Saddle your pony, let's ride together!
Saddle your pony, let's ride together!
Saddle your pony, let's ride together!
Ride to the reading circle!

(Repeat the verses until your young cowhands are rounded up in the reading area.)

Once everyone is ready to read, share *Just Like My Dad.*

LEARNING LINKS

—Language Arts

The young cowpoke in the story likes working with his dad. Ask your students to share special things they like to do with their dads as you record key words from their responses on a sheet of chart paper. Invite each child to make a special card for her father. Provide her with a 7" x 11" piece of construction paper. Have her fold it in half widthwise and then fold it in half again lengthwise. (It will look like a greeting card and fit in a letter-size envelope.) Have each child decorate the outside of her card with stickers, a drawing, or a sponge-painted design. Then ask her to write a message inside about something special she likes to do with her father. Older students may copy words from the chart, while younger ones can dictate their messages for you to print. Help each child put her card in an envelope, seal it, and add her father's name. Send these love notes home for little ones to share and dads to enjoy!

I mow the grass with my dad.

41

ART SMARTS

Gather round the campfire with some miniature marshmallows, and you've got the makings of an art project! Ask each child the name of her father. Using a felt pen, print her father's first name in large letters on a piece of tagboard. (Some children may not know their fathers' first names, so be prepared to write "Daddy" a few times!) Provide miniature marshmallows and direct each child to lick and then stick one end of a marshmallow onto the first letter. Continue, one letter at a time, until the name is "printed" in marshmallows!

PURPOSEFUL PLAY

During outdoor play, encourage some of the children to role-play cowboys and cowgirls and some to be cattle. Have the cowboys and cowgirls herd the cattle into different areas of the playground. After the roundup, have children switch roles and start the heart-healthy play all over again!

STORYBOOK CAFÉ

After a long day on the range, your cowpokes will enjoy hot corn muffins smothered in jam! Make a muffin for Dad, too!

Cowpoke Corn Pone

Supplies:
muffin tin
muffin tin liners
disposable bowls
plastic spoons
measuring spoons

Ingredients for each child:
1/2 tsp. sugar
2 tsp. cornmeal
2 tbsp. biscuit mix
1 tbsp. milk
4 tsp. Egg Beaters®
jam

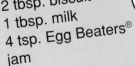

To make one muffin:
1. Measure and mix the first five ingredients in a bowl.
2. Spoon the batter into a liner set inside a muffin tin.
3. If you're making a muffin for your dad, too, repeat Steps 1 and 2.
4. Bake all the muffins at 375 degrees for 12 to 15 minutes.
5. Spread with jam and chow down!

HAZEL'S AMAZING MOTHER

Written & Illustrated by Rosemary Wells

When Hazel takes a wrong turn and ends up in the hands of bullies, who will help her?
Her mother is on the far side of town—but you'll be amazed at what Hazel's mother can do!

READING CIRCLE

Ask students to join you in the reading circle by singing this song to the tune of "Are You Sleeping?"

Where is Hazel?	Where is Hazel?
Where is Hazel?	Where is Hazel?
She is lost.	She is lost.
She is lost.	She is lost.
Who will help to find her?	Come to reading circle.
Who will help to find her?	Come to reading circle.
Come and see.	Read with me.
Come and see.	Read with me.

(Repeat the verses until all your youngsters have gathered in the reading circle.)

When your students are set for a story, read aloud *Hazel's Amazing Mother*.

 ## LEARNING LINKS

—Language Arts

Do your children have special stories to share about their amazing mothers? After reading the story, invite each child in a small group to sit in your teacher's chair and tell his story to the group. Then ask students to think about all the special things mothers do. Make a list of their ideas on chart paper. Provide older children with colored pencils, crayons, and paper. Have them draw pictures of things their amazing mothers do. Invite them to write words under each picture or dictate as you write. Ask younger students to clip pictures from magazines to represent things their moms do. Have them glue the pictures to pieces of paper; then add their dictation. Gather each child's pictures into a book, add a personalized cover, and staple. Moms will be amazed when they see these projects!

ART SMARTS

These child-drawn portraits of moms are sure to become treasured keepsakes! Ask each child to close her eyes and think about her mother's face. What color is her hair? Is it long or short, curly or straight? What color are her eyes? Does she wear earrings or a necklace? Provide children with large pieces of construction paper and crayons. Ask each child to draw a large picture of her mother's face on a sheet of construction paper.

Prepare a frame for each child's picture. Simply cut the center from another sheet of construction paper in the child's choice of colors (see illustration). Provide a heart-shaped hole puncher and invite each child to take a turn punching heart shapes all over her paper frame. Use strategically placed dots of glue to adhere the frame over the portrait, making sure the corners are secured. Display these masterpieces on a bulletin board in your classroom with the title "Our Amazing Mothers!" After visitors have a chance to admire them, send them home for moms to keep.

PURPOSEFUL PLAY

In your dramatic-play center, provide props for acting out the story of *Hazel's Amazing Mother*. You might include a baby carriage, a doll, a soccer ball, a picnic basket, and a blanket. If your young actors and actresses wish, have groups perform the story for neighboring classes.

STORYBOOK CAFÉ

Her mother makes sure Hazel doesn't leave home without a kiss! Little ones will enjoy making and eating these kisses. Have each child make one for his mother, too!

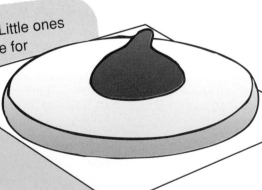

Cookie Kisses
(makes 52)

Supplies:
cookie sheets
spatula
table knife

Ingredients:
2 rolls of refrigerated sugar cookie dough
13-oz. bag of Hershey's® Kisses® candies

To make cookie kisses:
1. Cut each roll of cookie dough into 13 even slices. Then cut each slice in half.
2. Roll a half slice of dough into a ball and place it on a cookie sheet.
3. Bake all cookies at 375 degrees for eight minutes or until lightly browned.
4. Immediately press an unwrapped candy into the center of each cookie.
5. Cool and eat or share with Mom!

MA DEAR'S APRONS

Written by Patricia C. McKissack
Illustrated by Floyd Cooper

How does David Earl know which day of the week it is? By the color of the apron his mother wears, that's how! Meet David Earl and his Ma Dear in this depiction of turn-of-the-century Southern life.

READING CIRCLE

Bring your children skipping to the reading circle by singing these verses to the tune of "Skip to My Lou."

Ma Dear washes clothes on Monday.
Ma Dear washes clothes on Monday.
Ma Dear washes clothes on Monday.
She wears a blue apron.

Ma Dear irons clothes on Tuesday.
Ma Dear irons clothes on Tuesday.
Ma Dear irons clothes on Tuesday.
She wears a yellow apron.

What does Ma Dear do on Wednesday?
What color apron does she wear?
Skip, skip, skip to our circle.
You'll find the answer there!

(Repeat the last two lines until all your little ones have gathered in the reading circle.)

When your students are ready to read, share *Ma Dear's Aprons*.

LEARNING LINKS

—Social Studies

Following the story, help the children recall what Ma Dear does each day and the color of the apron she wears. Do their mothers or other family members do some of the same things? Who washes the clothes in their family? Does anyone iron clothes? Who cooks and who cleans? Lead the children to compare how things were done at the turn of the century and how we do things now. Do we wash our clothes the same way that Ma Dear does? Do we take a bath the same way that David Earl does?

After your discussion, provide seven large pieces of butcher paper. Cut six into apron shapes and one into a dress shape. Label each apron with a day of the week and label the dress "Sunday"; then draw a line down the center of each to divide it into two sections. Beginning with Monday's apron, ask student volunteers to tell what Ma Dear does on that day. List her activity on one side of the apron. Then ask volunteers to list things their parents do on the other side of the apron. Continue with the other five aprons and the dress. Then divide the class into seven groups and ask the members of each group to illustrate the tasks listed on each shape. Display the six aprons and the dress in sequence on a bulletin board or wall.

45

ART SMARTS

David Earl likes to hear Madam Pearlie's singing. Play a recording of spiritual or folk music and invite youngsters to try out this creative activity as they listen. Provide each child with a large piece of brown kraft paper (cut up paper grocery bags, if you like). Direct students to paint a light coat of liquid starch on their papers; then have them use colored chalk to draw designs inspired by the music. Allow the starch to dry completely before displaying these creations.

PURPOSEFUL PLAY

David Earl tries hard to say the tongue twister Ma Dear teaches him, and your little ones will enjoy trying to say some tongue twisters, too. Reread the one Ma Dear teaches David Earl; then invite youngsters to echo each line after you, trying to do it faster each time. Then try these tongue twisters. Can your students say each of these five times fast?

Six sticky sucker sticks.
Inchworms itching.
Fat frogs flying past fast.
A noisy noise annoys an oyster.
Friendly Frank flips fine flapjacks.
Toy boat. Toy boat. Toy boat.

STORYBOOK CAFÉ

After the apples are peeled for this treat, invite each child to take a longer piece of apple peel and throw it over his shoulder. According to Ma Dear's game, it will form the first letter of the name of someone who loves him!

Appleskedaddle Sauce
(makes 12 servings)

Supplies:
vegetable peeler
knife
tablespoon
measuring cup
saucepan and hot plate *or* electric frying pan
cups and spoons for serving

Ingredients:
6 apples
1¼ cups water
4 tbsp. honey
cinnamon

To make appleskedaddle sauce:
1. Peel, core, and slice apples.
2. Put apple slices and water in a saucepan or electric frying pan.
3. Cover and cook until tender (about 20 to 30 minutes).
4. Add honey and cinnamon.
5. Cool a bit and eat. Then skedaddle outside to play!

ANIMAL DADS

Written by Sneed B. Collard III
Illustrated by Steve Jenkins

All dads are not alike. There are helpful dads, playful dads, and even animal dads!

READING CIRCLE

Pack up your students and head out on a safari to visit fathers in the animal kingdom with this song sung to the tune of "The Wheels on the Bus."

The wheels on our bus	What kind of animals	The brakes on our bus
Go round and round,	Will we see,	Go squeaky-squeak,
Round and round,	Will we see,	Squeaky-squeak,
Round and round.	Will we see?	Squeaky-squeak.
The wheels on our bus	What kind of animals	The brakes on our bus
Go round and round.	Will we see	Go squeaky-squeak,
Let's go on safari!	On our safari?	Stopping at our reading circle!

(Lead youngsters in a line around the room as you sing. Stop in your reading area and invite everyone to sit down.)

Once all your safari-bound students are seated, read aloud *Animal Dads*.

 ## LEARNING LINKS

—Science

After reading the story, ask children to think about the animal dad that they liked the most. Can they remember one of the special things this animal dad does for his children? Ask each child to share her favorite animal dad and what she remembers from the book. (Revisit pages as necessary.) Next, explain that when people go on a trip or safari, they often take pictures and make a scrapbook. Provide each child with a half sheet of white copy paper and crayons so that she can make a picture of her favorite animal dad. Have the book available for children who need to refer to the pictures. Collect the finished pictures and mount each one on a sheet of construction paper. Use the space below each picture to add a label and write the "photographer's" dictation about it. Children will enjoy reading their "Safari Scrapbook of Animal Dads" over and over again!

Shelley

Lion

The daddy lion is tired because he guards the babies.

ART SMARTS

Ask the children to look closely at the pictures in *Animal Dads*. The illustrations are made with many different kinds of paper. Provide children with a variety of papers, such as construction paper, tissue paper, brown bag paper, wallpaper samples, shredded paper, wrapping paper, and waxed paper. Also supply white glue and scissors. Invite each child to tear or cut shapes from a variety of papers and then glue them in layers on a large piece of construction paper. The torn or cut shapes may form an animal dad found in the story or simply a beautiful paper collage. Just like dads, each work of art will be different!

PURPOSEFUL PLAY

Your little ones may enjoy acting out the roles of some of the animal dads in the story, such as the vole, killdeer, salmon, wolf, and lion. As you reread the pages featuring each of these animals, invite the children to imitate the animal dad. Can they dig an underground nest like the prairie vole? Can they pretend to have a broken wing like the killdeer and lead the fox away from the eggs? Can they leap and wriggle like a salmon? Can they hunt and howl like a wolf? Finish this activity by having little ones lie down and take a nap like the lion!

STORYBOOK CAFÉ

Help some bird dads (and moms) who gather food for their young ones by mixing up a batch of this pudding.

Birdie Pudding

Supplies:
large bowl
mixing spoon
measuring cup
pinecones
pipe cleaners
waxed paper

Ingredients:
1 pound of lard
2 cups of peanut butter
dry oatmeal

To make birdie pudding:
1. Mix the lard and peanut butter in a big bowl.
2. Add as much oatmeal as you can without making the pudding too dry.
3. Wrap a pipe cleaner around the top of a pinecone. Then stick the cone in the pudding and spread lots of pudding all over it.
4. Set the cone on waxed paper. If desired, sprinkle some additional oatmeal over it.
5. Hang the pinecones in a tree or place them high in a tall bush.

BUNNY CAKES

Written & Illustrated by Rosemary Wells

It's Grandma's birthday, and Max and Ruby are both busy making special cakes for her. When Ruby sends Max shopping for her angel cake's ingredients, he finds a creative way to get decorations for his earthworm cake as well.

READING CIRCLE

Ask youngsters to join you in the reading circle by chanting these verses to the rhythm of "Pat-a-Cake."

> *Bunny Cakes, Bunny Cakes,* come and read.
> This is a funny book, indeed!
> Max and Ruby are making cakes
> For Grandma's birthday. Let's see what it takes!

(Repeat until all your little bunnies have hopped into the reading circle.)

Once everyone is settled, read aloud *Bunny Cakes.*

LEARNING LINKS

—Language Arts

Max and Ruby certainly have their own notions about making the perfect cake for Grandma. Find out how your little bakers would go about this task. To prepare, cut a large cake shape from bulletin board paper. Then don a chef's hat and apron and ask youngsters to tell you the steps for making a birthday cake. Review some of the ingredients used by Ruby to get them thinking. Then record their dictated steps on the paper cake, taking opportunities to point out letters, sight words, and punctuation as you write. Review the finished recipe and post it in your classroom. It's bound to bring chuckles from classroom visitors! If desired, close this activity by serving up slices of Ruby's special angel surprise cake with raspberry-fluff icing. (Store-bought angel food cake with pink-tinted vanilla icing will do!)

Birthday Cake

1. Put 16 cups of flour in a bowl.
2. Crack 10 eggs. Throw out the shells.
3. Pour in 4 cups of milk.
4. Stir it up.
5. Bake it at 500 degrees for 6 hours.
6. Add frosting and candles.

ART SMARTS

Stir up some creativity in your little chefs by having them make pretend cakes for their own grandparents. To prepare, make a few copies of the cake pattern on page 51 on tagboard. Cut these out for children to use as tracers. Then duplicate the recipe card for each child. Provide construction paper, stickers, markers, stamps, and stamp pads. Direct each child to trace a cake onto her choice of construction paper; then have her cut out her cake. Encourage her to decorate her cake with the art materials of her choice. Then have her draw the ingredients she would use in baking the cake on her copy of the recipe card. Have her write or dictate the name of each item. Glue each child's finished cake and recipe card to a separate sheet of 12" x 18" construction paper; then invite all your little ones to send their creations to their grandparents.

PURPOSEFUL PLAY

Set up a baking center in your classroom for youngsters to enjoy. Provide measuring cups and spoons, mixing bowls, muffin tins, cookie sheets, cake pans, spatulas, wooden spoons, aprons, and oven mitts. If desired, place the items near a sand or water table, so little ones can do some real measuring. Invite them to share their observations about the various measuring utensils. What a fun way to combine math and dramatic play!

STORYBOOK CAFÉ

Your students will find these treats as delightful as Max's grandma found the earthworm cake!

Earthworm Dirt Cups
(makes 20)

Supplies:
mixing bowl
wire whisk
measuring cup
clear plastic cups
plastic spoons

Ingredients:
two 6-oz. packages instant chocolate pudding
6 cups milk
one 12-oz. container whipped topping, thawed
1 package chocolate sandwich cookies, crushed
40 Gummy Worm® candies

To make earthworm dirt cups:
1. Mix pudding and milk according to package directions.
2. For each snack, layer three to four spoonfuls of pudding, three to four spoonfuls of whipped topping, and three to four spoonfuls of crushed cookies in a plastic cup. Repeat layers.
3. Decorate each snack with two Gummy Worms.

Cake Pattern
Use with "Art Smarts" on page 50.

Recipe Card
Use with "Art Smarts" on page 50.

From the kitchen of _____

Here's a yummy cake for you, with a recipe that's new.

It's one I made up by myself. Are these items on your shelf?

Hang my cake for all to see; it's sure to make you think of me!

DEAR ANNIE

Written & Illustrated by Judith Caseley

When Annie was born, Grandpa sent her a card with a picture of a rose on it. And he's been her special pen pal ever since.

READING CIRCLE

Call youngsters to your reading circle with this song sung to the tune of "A-Tisket A-Tasket."

Dear Annie, Dear Annie,
Come, let's read Dear Annie.
Who wrote a letter to this girl?
Who was her special pen pal?

(Repeat the verse until all your students have gathered in the reading circle.)

Once your students are ready for storytime, read aloud *Dear Annie.*

LEARNING LINKS

—Language Arts

Encourage your little ones to write letters to their own grandparent (or older adult) pen pals. In advance, ask parents to send in stamped envelopes addressed to grandparents (or older family friends). To get your young-sters started on their letters, make a large chart with two columns, labeled "Things to Ask" and "Things to Tell." Help your students brainstorm ideas for each column. Next, ask an older elementary class to act as writing buddies for your youngsters. Pair each of your students with an older child, and ask each older helper to write her buddy's dictated message, using original ideas or ones from the chart. Be sure to have older students review the finished notes to be sure they've included everything little ones want to say. Mail the letters. Then invite students to bring in response letters they receive to post on a bulletin board similar to the one Annie's class made in the story.

ART SMARTS

If your little ones are delighted by the cards they receive from classmates on Valentine's Day, they'll love receiving mail at other times of the year! Just have each child decorate a box (such as a pencil box or tall tissue box) to serve as her mailbox. Have each child keep her mailbox on her desk or in her cubby. Stock your writing center with stationery, envelopes, postcards, greeting cards, and writing tools. Add a simple word list with reference words students might refer to when writing letters. Encourage all your little ones to write notes and letters during writing time or center time; then have them deliver their correspondence to classmates' mailboxes. Be sure to have a mailbox for yourself, too!

PURPOSEFUL PLAY

Extend your letter-writing fun (see "Art Smarts") by creating a class post office to encourage dramatic play. Each day, assign two students to act as clerks and one to be the mail carrier. Provide a toy cash register, old stamps (or new stickers), ink pads, and rubber stamps. When a student finishes a letter, have her take it to the classroom post office where she can purchase a stamp and have her envelope rubber-stamped and sorted by the clerk on duty. The mail carrier will put the letter in his mailbag (a canvas tote bag) to be delivered at a designated time to the recipient.

STORYBOOK CAFÉ

These edible pencils have the "write" stuff for snacktime!

Pretzel Pencils

Supplies:
hot plate (or microwave)
small saucepan (or microwave-safe bowl)
large spoon
plastic or Styrofoam® bowls
paper plates

Ingredients:
6-oz. bag chocolate chips
1 tbsp. butter
1 bag pretzel rods
toppings such as crushed peanuts, mini chocolate chips, or candy sprinkles

To make chocolate sauce:
1. Melt chocolate chips and butter over medium heat or in microwave for one minute on high. Stir.

To make a pretzel pencil:
1. Dip a pretzel rod in chocolate sauce to create eraser end of pencil.
2. Roll in desired topping.
3. Allow the finished pencil to sit for five to ten minutes as the chocolate sets.
4. Enjoy while writing a letter to a pen pal!

SONG AND DANCE MAN

Written by Karen Ackerman
Illustrated by Stephen Gammell

When Grandpa does his vaudeville act for his grandchildren in the attic, it's a show they'll never forget!

READING CIRCLE

Hold up a copy of *Song and Dance Man*. Then invite little ones to your reading circle with this song sung to the tune of "This Old Man."

This old man, he could tap,
He could tap wearing a cap!
With a tip-tap, paddywhack,
Come on over here.
Watch him dance and give a cheer!

This old man, he could sing,
He told jokes and everything!
With a tip-tap, paddywhack,
Come on over here.
Hear his jokes and give a cheer!

(Repeat the verses until all your students have tip-tapped into your reading area.)

Once all your youngsters are in the reading circle, read aloud *Song and Dance Man*.

LEARNING LINKS

Math

Put problem-solving skills in the spotlight with this fun activity! For each child, duplicate page 56 onto white construction paper. Instruct each student to color and then cut out the song and dance man and all his clothing. (Precut the pieces for younger students.) Then challenge her to find eight different ways to dress him for his vaudeville show. After students have discovered eight combinations, have each child glue her favorite outfit onto Grandpa. Display the completed characters on a black bulletin board with a yellow spotlight.

ART SMARTS

If youngsters want others to view their vaudeville show, they'll need to make posters to advertise. Provide each student in a small group with a sheet of construction paper. Show youngsters a model poster you've made, pointing out the picture of the performer and words that tell about the act. Then ask older students to draw pictures of themselves performing their vaudeville acts. Write each child's dictation as he describes his act. For younger students, take an instant photo of each child wearing his costume. Glue the photo to his construction paper and add his dictation about his act. Display the completed posters near your classroom vaudeville stage.

See Tyler Sing and Dance With a Cane

He's Good!

PURPOSEFUL PLAY

You may not be able to visit a real vaudeville stage, but you can have one in your own classroom! Bring in an old trunk (or a cardboard box decorated to resemble one) and fill it with a variety of men's hats, ties, vests, and shoes, as well as some dancing canes (check your local party-supply store). Invite little ones to dress up and make up dances or songs for their own vaudeville acts. Be sure to have a full-length mirror available where your young dancers and singers can check out their performances. Then set aside a time when children may (if they wish) perform their acts for classmates.

STORYBOOK CAFÉ

Students will be tap dancing over these delicious cookies!

Dancing Man Cookies
(makes 12–15 large cookies)

Supplies:
rolling pin
gingerbread man cookie cutters
plastic knives
oven
cookie sheet

Ingredients:
flour
1 roll refrigerated sugar cookie dough
frosting
assorted decorating goodies, such as sprinkles, M&M's® brand mini baking bits, mini chocolate chips, and shredded coconut
black string licorice

To make dancing man cookies:
1. Preheat oven to 350°.
2. Roll out cookie dough on floured surface.
3. Press cookie cutter into dough. Place cookies on cookie sheet.
4. Bake cookies according to package directions.
5. Allow to cool; then frost.
6. Decorate as desired.
7. Press a three-inch length of string licorice onto one of the cookie man's hands to make a cane.

Theme: GRANDPARENTS

Grandpa Pattern and Clothing
Use with "Learning Links" on page 54.

THE TUB GRANDFATHER

Written by Pam Conrad
Illustrated by Richard Egiclski

The Tub People discover the family grandfather, Walter, lying in the dust beneath the radiator. But it takes some special memories to rouse him from his sleep and help him rejoin the family.

READING CIRCLE

Encourage little ones to join you for storytime with this song sung to the tune of "The Itsy Bitsy Spider."

Come and hear a story about a man of wood.
His family loved him and did all that they could
To wake him up from a dusty sleep so long,
So he could be with his family—
Right where he belongs!

(Repeat the song until all your youngsters have joined the reading circle.)

When all your students are ready for storytime, read aloud *The Tub Grandfather.*

LEARNING LINKS

—Math

Combine a math lesson with a tasty snack for this activity. Provide each child in a small group with a "tub" (a small rectangular box, such as a butter box or a check box) and eight Teddy Grahams® to represent the eight Tub People. Pose several story problems involving the Tub People, such as "The Tub Child and the Doctor were in the tub. The Tub Mother and the Grandfather joined them. How many Tub People were in the tub?" Encourage students to use their Teddy Grahams to figure out the answers. Save some subtraction problems for the end of this activity, and invite students to eat up the answers!

ART SMARTS

Invite each of your youngsters to create a paper portrait of one of the Tub People. Provide each artist in a small group with a six-inch circle cut from skin-toned construction paper and access to the book for reference. Then supply construction paper, scissors, crayons, and glue. Have each child cut shapes from the construction paper to create the features of one of the Tub People, such as the Grandfather's hat, mustache, cheeks, eyebrows, and bow tie. Invite youngsters to use crayons to add details such as eyes or stripes. Display the finished portraits lined up on a bulletin board—just as the Tub People line up on the windowsill in the story.

PURPOSEFUL PLAY

Everyone loves a parade and the Tub People are no exception! Hold a parade of your own and invite students to join in the fun. Pair students and invite each pair to think of a unique way to march. They might march on tiptoe, sideways, or add movements with their arms. Then play some lively music and let the parade begin! Lead your partner parade around the school and encourage youngsters to show off their creative movements.

STORYBOOK CAFÉ

Memories of the Tub Grandmother's field of flowers helped awaken the Tub Grandfather. Make your own flowery fields that little ones will remember as a tasty snack!

Field of Flowers

Supplies:
napkins
plastic knives or craft sticks

Ingredients:
1 round sugar cookie per child
green-tinted vanilla frosting
flower-shaped cake sprinkles

To make a field of flowers:
1. Spread green frosting on cookie.
2. Sprinkle on flower-shaped sprinkles.
3. Enjoy!

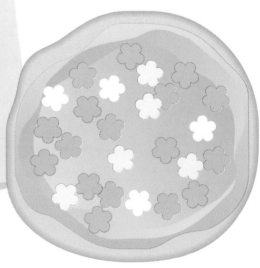

THE BAG I'M TAKING TO GRANDMA'S

Written by Shirley Neitzel
Illustrated by Nancy Winslow Parker

What's a young boy to pack for a trip to Grandma's house? Just what's absolutely necessary: a baseball mitt, toy cars, a space shuttle, wooden animals… Of course, Mom might have something to say about his selections!

READING CIRCLE

Bid your little ones to pack up and join you in the reading circle by singing this song to the tune of "If You're Happy and You Know It." Hold up the book so youngsters can see its cover.

If you're going to Grandma's house,
What should you take?
If you're going to Grandma's house,
What should you take?
Toy cars, a baseball mitt,
A book to read, or clothes that fit?
If you're going to Grandma's house,
What should you take?

Let's read about this boy
Who packs his bag.
Let's read about this boy
Who packs his bag.
Will he take all of this stuff?
Or will Mom say, "That's enough"?
Let's read about this boy
Who packs his bag.

(Repeat the last verse until all your students have gathered for storytime.)

Once your youngsters are settled in the reading circle, read aloud *The Bag I'm Taking to Grandma's.*

LEARNING LINKS

—Science

Strengthen students' classification skills with this packing activity. Bring a suitcase to circle time, along with a few articles of clothing, some musical instruments, and some toys. Announce to students that you are taking your own trip to Grandma's house. Ask them to help you sort the items before you pack. Have youngsters survey the collection of items and come up with categories by which to sort. Then pack the sorted items in separate sections of the suitcase. After this group activity, give each child a copy of page 61 to complete on his own.

ART SMARTS

If your students seem to have a handle on packing, invite them to pack their own bags. In advance, cut a few suitcase shapes from tagboard to use as tracers. Ask each child to trace and cut out a suitcase from a large sheet of white construction paper. (Precut the suitcases for younger children.) Ask each youngster to consider the climate he'd be visiting if he went to visit his grandmother (or another relative). Then have older students draw and label items they need to pack in their suitcases. For younger children, provide magazines and encourage them to cut out and glue on pictures of items they should pack. Compile the completed pages into a class book, with a colored construction paper cover and back cut to match the pages.

Share the book at a group time; then add it to your reading center for little ones to enjoy on their own.

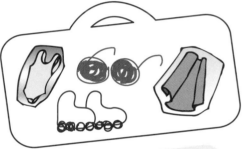

PURPOSEFUL PLAY

This center will get your youngsters sorting and packing—pronto! Gather two sets of pictures (such as those found in travel magazines and brochures)—one that depicts cold climates and one that shows warm climates. Place the two sets of pictures in a center, along with two empty suitcases and a variety of items appropriate to each climate. Invite student pairs to visit this center. Have each child choose one set of pictures and a suitcase. Then have her sort through the items and pack the ones she'd need for a visit to her chosen climate. Challenge students to see which child in the pair can pack her bag faster!

STORYBOOK CAFÉ

These edible suitcases are packed with nutrition *and* fun!

Pack-Your-Bag Pita

Supplies:
sharp knife (for teacher use)
paper plates
serving spoon

Ingredients:
1 green pepper
1/2 pita round per child
tuna salad
shredded lettuce

pickle slices
cheese slices
tomato slices

To prepare the green pepper:
1. Slice the green pepper crosswise. Remove seeds and pith.
2. Cut each slice in half to make suitcase handles.

To make a pack-your-bag pita:
1. Fill a pita half with a large spoonful of tuna salad.
2. Pack your pita with your choice of additional ingredients.
3. Slip a green pepper piece into the opening of the pita to make the bag's handle.
4. Unpack your bag—right into your tummy!

Name _____

Suitcase Sorting

 Color.

 Cut.

Glue.

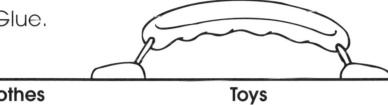

Clothes	Toys	Other

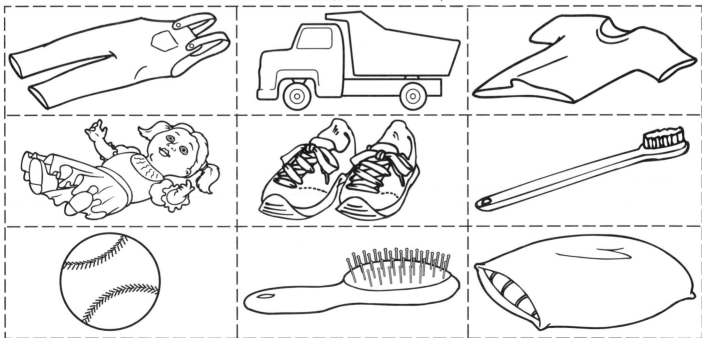

WHEN AUNT LENA DID THE RHUMBA

Written by Eileen Kurtis-Kleinman
Illustrated by Diane Greenseid

Sophie's Aunt Lena loves dancing and movie stars and especially the Broadway musical matinee every Wednesday. But when she sprains her ankle, she's stuck in bed with no more matinees for a while. Will Sophie think of a way to bring the matinee to Aunt Lena?

READING CIRCLE

Hold up your copy of *When Aunt Lena Did the Rhumba.* Then invite little ones to dance on over to your reading circle as you sing this song to the tune of "If You're Happy and You Know It."

Aunt Lena loves to see her Wednesday show.
Aunt Lena loves to see her Wednesday show.
Aunt Lena loves her show, but now she cannot go!
What will she do without her Wednesday show?

If you'd like to hear this book, come on over!
If you'd like to hear this book, come on over!
If you'd like to hear this book, then join me for a look!
If you'd like to hear this book, come on over!

(Repeat the last verse until all your students have gathered in your reading area.)

Once your youngsters are ready to read, share *When Aunt Lena Did the Rhumba.*

LEARNING LINKS

—Language Arts

Sophie enjoys spending time with her Aunt Lena. Invite your students to tell stories about their aunts. On a sheet of chart paper, record the names of the children's aunts as they tell about them. Then use the name chart to practice some language skills. Ask students to find names that begin with a particular letter or to look for names that begin or end with the same letter. Read aloud two names from the list. Ask children to tell you if the names begin with the same sound or different sounds.

Extend this activity by giving each child a small plastic bag of alphabet cereal. Call out a letter and point to it on your chart. Ask all the children to hunt for a matching cereal letter in their bags. If a child finds the correct match, invite her to eat it up!

Lisa	Susan
Betsy	Marjorie
Thelma	Anna
Adele	
Vivienne	
Bobbi	
Sarah	

ART SMARTS

As Aunt Lena would say, here's a "bee-yoo-tee-ful" idea! Encourage each child to make a theater poster featuring his favorite aunt (or uncle). Have each child use tempera paint to create a large picture of his aunt on a sheet of 12" x 18" white construction paper. Add his aunt's name with black tempera paint. After the paint dries, provide a shallow bowl of salad oil and a large, clean paintbrush. Ask him to brush the oil over his painting. When the oil dries, hang the posters in your classroom windows and watch these favorite relatives shine in the spotlight!

PURPOSEFUL PLAY

If you have aspiring actors, singers, or dancers in your class, they'll love putting on a show! Raid your dress-up box to find hats, jewelry, gloves, and perhaps a feather boa to use for costumes. Designate a stage area in your dramatic-play area. If possible, rig a stage curtain by hanging a bedsheet on a spring-loaded shower curtain rod or even over a tall chart stand. Visit the public library to find soundtracks from some famous Broadway musicals and spin them on your record player or pop them into your cassette player. Students visiting your dramatic-play center can rehearse and perform to their heart's content!

STORYBOOK CAFÉ

After eating this snack, your little ones will be shouting, "Encore! Encore!"

Cha-Cha Bars
(makes 12–20)

Supplies:
7" x 10³/₄" baking pan
mixing bowl
large, empty jar with lid
mixing spoon
measuring cup
measuring spoons
napkins
knife (for teacher use)

Ingredients:
shortening or butter to grease pan
1¹/₄ cups flour
1¹/₂ tsp. baking powder
¹/₂ tsp. salt
2 eggs
¹/₂ cup sugar
¹/₂ cup oil
¹/₂ cup orange juice
powdered sugar

To make cha-cha bars:
1. Preheat oven to 375°. Grease the baking pan.
2. Stir together flour, baking powder, and salt in the mixing bowl.
3. Crack the two eggs into the jar.
4. Add the sugar, oil, and orange juice to the eggs. Put on the lid.
5. Cha-cha around the room as you shake the jar about 30 times.
6. Add the flour mixture to the jar, replace the lid, and keep dancing and shaking until the mixture is smooth.
7. Pour the batter into the pan and bake for about 20 minutes.
8. Cool and cut into bars of desired size.
9. Serve each bar with a sprinkle of powdered sugar.

THE GARDENER

Written by Sarah Stewart
Illustrated by David Small

When Lydia Grace's family falls on hard times, she goes to live with her unsmiling Uncle Jim in a big gray city. Lydia Grace's talent for gardening gradually brightens up Uncle Jim's bakery. Will her rooftop surprise manage to bring a smile to his face?

READING CIRCLE

Call your youngsters to the reading circle with these verses sung to the tune of "Go Tell Aunt Rhody."

Go tell Uncle Jim.
Go tell Uncle Jim.
Go tell Uncle Jim.
That Lydia Grace is coming.

She's traveling by train.
She's traveling by train.
She's traveling by train.
To live with Uncle Jim.

Can she make him smile?
Can she make him smile?
Can she make him smile?
Join our circle and see!

(Repeat the last verse until all your little ones are in the reading circle.)

When your smiling students are ready for the story, read aloud *The Gardener.*

 LEARNING LINKS

—Math

How many of your students have uncles? Find out with this simple graphing activity. Divide a sheet of chart paper into two columns, labeled "Yes" and "No." Give each child a sticky dot. Ask, "Do you have an uncle?" Direct each child, in turn, to put her sticky dot in the appropriate column of the chart to answer your question. Count up the results for each column and compare the two numbers. Then invite little ones to share information or stories about their uncles.

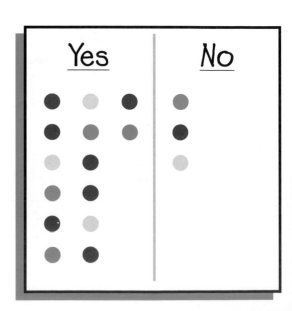

—*Science*

Turn your classroom into a beautiful garden with some inspiration from Lydia Grace! First, have each student bring from home an interesting container, such as a teacup or an old cake pan. Ask some parent helpers to provide you with some fast-growing seeds (such as nasturtiums or marigolds), a flat or two of starter plants, and some potting soil. Invite each child to plant a few seeds and/or a baby plant in her container. Provide water and sunlight and soon your little gardeners will have your classroom in full bloom!

ART SMARTS

Flip back through the book, and ask youngsters to look closely at David Small's illustrations, particularly the double-page picture of Lydia Grace in the dark train station. Can they see the impression of texture in the background? Invite them to imitate this art technique by doing some rubbings. Collect a variety of leaves, seed pods, and unopened seed packets. Then cover a table with a thick layer of newspaper and set out some newsprint and peeled crayons. Encourage a young artist to choose a few plant items to arrange on top of the newspaper in her work area. Then have her place a sheet of newsprint over the items and rub across the paper with a crayon. Ta da!

STORYBOOK CAFÉ

These cakes are sure to bring one thousand smiles!

Flower Cakes

Supplies:
plastic knives or craft sticks
paper plates
decorating tips for tubes of icing

Ingredients:
1 graham cracker per child
container of white frosting
tubes of decorator icing

To make a flower cake:
1. Frost a graham cracker (cake) with some of the white frosting.
2. Use tubes of decorator icing with tips to add flowers and other designs.

JUST RIGHT STEW

Written by Karen English
Illustrated by Anna Rich

It's Big Mama's birthday and Victoria's mama and Aunt Rose are cooking up a special dinner. But can they get the stew to taste like Big Mama's? Only Victoria and Big Mama know the secret ingredient!

READING CIRCLE

Sing this song to the tune of "Happy Birthday to You" to call your students to the circle and stir up some reading fun!

It's Big Mama's birthday.	Will they get it just right?
It's Big Mama's birthday.	Will they get it just right?
Her family's making stew,	Let's read and find out
'Cause it's Big Mama's birthday!	If they get it just right!

(Repeat the verses until all your youngsters have joined the reading circle.)

Once everyone is seated in the circle, read aloud *Just Right Stew.*

 LEARNING LINKS

—Social Studies

After sharing the story, ask students if they can remember the names of the aunts, the great-aunt, and the cousin in the story. Ask them to share stories about family gatherings when many relatives get together. Then invite each child to show off some of his family members with the reproducible on page 68. In advance, ask parents to send in photos showing some of their child's relatives, such as aunts, uncles, or cousins. (Tell parents that the photos may be trimmed, and ask them to label the photo with their child's name.) Give each student a copy of page 68. Invite him to color the face to resemble himself. Then glue or tape the photo of his relatives in the space provided. Ask him to dictate a sentence or two about the relatives shown in the picture as you write his words in the speech bubble. Display the finished papers on a bulletin board or bind them together in a class book titled "Our Extended Family."

ART SMARTS

Your youngsters may not be familiar with some of the herbs and spices mentioned in the story. Invite them to find out about the herbs' appearances, textures, and scents with this free-form art project. Visit the grocery store spice aisle and purchase some dill, lemon pepper, cumin, garlic powder, and red pepper (or ask some parent helpers to provide them). Also provide some salt and sugar. Encourage each artist to drizzle some glue onto a sheet of construction paper to make an interesting design. Then have her sprinkle sugar, salt, or her choice of spices over the glue. Allow the glue to dry; then shake off the excess spice. Save the leftovers to make some just right stew (see "Storybook Café").

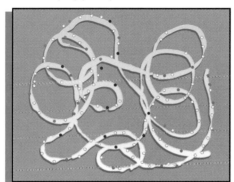

PURPOSEFUL PLAY

Young chefs-in-the-making will love cooking up some stew in your water table! Provide a big basket or grocery bag full of play food, as well as some old salt-shakers or glitter bottles full of colored sand to represent spices and herbs. Add some spoons, ladles, aprons, and plastic bowls, and your youngsters will take it from there!

STORYBOOK CAFÉ

Before preparing this stew, ask each child's family to send in a vegetable from home that's been prepared for stew (such as a peeled and cut carrot or a small can of peas). While you are cooking, assign the roles of Mama, Aunt Violet, Aunt Clary, Great-Aunt Mae, and Victoria. Have those characters add the ingredients as instructed in the recipe.

Just Right Stew

Supplies:
soup pot
can opener
measuring spoons
mixing spoon
ladle
plastic bowls
plastic spoons

Ingredients:
one 32-oz. carton chicken broth
   for every 8–10 vegetables
vegetables
dill
cumin
lemon pepper
1/4 tsp. garlic powder

red pepper flakes
sugar to taste
3–5 tbsp. flour

To make just right stew:
1. Pour the chicken broth into the soup pot. Add the prepared vegetables.
2. Have Mama add a pinch of dill and a pinch of lemon pepper to the pot.
3. Have Aunt Violet add a pinch of cumin.
4. Have Aunt Clary add the garlic powder.
5. Have Great-Aunt Mae add just a *few* flakes of red pepper.
6. Have Victoria add the secret ingredient—sugar! (Start with one tablespoon.)
7. Bring to a boil; then simmer over medium-low heat for one hour or until all the vegetables are soft.
8. Stir the flour into a little water to make a thin paste. Add this to the pot and stir to thicken a bit and achieve a stew consistency.

Attach photo here.

MUSIC OVER MANHATTAN

Written by Mark Karlins
Illustrated by Jack E. Davis

Poor Bernie. It wasn't much fun being cousin to the smart and talented Herbert. But Uncle Louie helps Bernie discover his musical talent, and pretty soon he's floating on air!

READING CIRCLE

Encourage little ones to march on over to your reading area as you sing this song to the tune of "When the Saints Go Marching In."

> Oh, will you come
> To our reading circle?
> Oh, will you come
> To our reading circle?
> Come hear how Bernie learns the trumpet
> In our reading circle today!

(Repeat the song until all your students have gathered in your reading circle.)

Once youngsters are seated, read aloud *Music Over Manhattan*.

LEARNING LINKS

—Character Building

Flip back through the book and look at the expressions on Bernie's face at the beginning of the story and then at the end. Learning to play "Moonlight Over Manhattan" after all his hard work and practice must have made him very happy! Ask youngsters to think about things they can do that make them feel proud. Then ask them to name some things they'd like to learn. Will they have to practice to achieve their goals?

After your discussion, provide magazines, scissors, glue, and paper. Invite youngsters to find pictures that show things they can already do and things they'd like to learn. Have each youngster glue the pictures to her paper to make a collage. Have her finish her collage by squirting a line of glue all around the perimeter, then adding a fancy yarn border. Display the collages on a bulletin board titled "Talents and Dreams" and add some shiny paper stars for a special effect!

69

ART SMARTS

When Uncle Louie blew into his trumpet, the pigeons strutted and cooed! Your little ones may not be able to make such pleasing sounds, but they can blow their way to some beautiful artwork! Give each child a piece of white construction paper and a straw. Provide several small bowls of tempera paint in various colors, with a plastic spoon in each bowl. Have each child drop a bit of the paint color of her choice onto her paper. Then have her blow through her straw to make the paint move and create an interesting shape. Then have her repeat the process with other colors of paint. These windblown designs will soar through your classroom! Why, even the pencils will dance!

PURPOSEFUL PLAY

Compose a center where youngsters can make their own musical instruments. Try some of these ideas or add your own or your students'.

— Provide boxes or canisters with tight-fitting lids, a bowlful of rice or beans, and a scoop so youngsters can create shakers.

— Provide small boxes without lids and rubber bands. Little ones can stretch a few bands around a box to make a stringed instrument.

— Add cardboard tubes that can be decorated and tapped together like rhythm sticks. Lengths of dowel also make good rhythm sticks. Or they can be used as drumsticks with a plastic-container or box drum.

— Supply new plastic combs with waxed paper so little ones can hum a few bars!

STORYBOOK CAFÉ

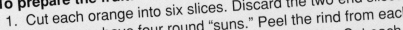

The oranges and bananas in this salad will brighten snacktime, like "so many small suns and moons"!

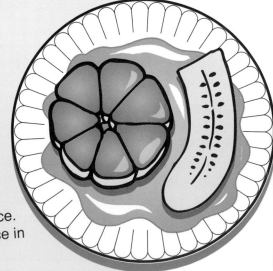

Sun and Moon Salad
(serves 20)

Supplies:
sharp knife (for teacher use)
tablespoon
plastic plates
plastic spoons

Ingredients:
5 oranges
5 bananas
five 8-oz. containers fruit yogurt
(in various flavors)

To prepare the fruit:
1. Cut each orange into six slices. Discard the two end slices, so that you have four round "suns." Peel the rind from each slice.
2. Peel each banana; then cut it in half lengthwise. Cut each piece in half crosswise so that you have four "moons."

To make sun and moon salad:
1. Put two tablespoons of yogurt on a paper plate and spread it out to create a background "sky."
2. Add an orange sun and a banana moon to the sky.
3. Watch as this salad flies right off the plate and into your mouth!

THE KEEPING QUILT

Written and Illustrated by Patricia Polacco

"We will make a quilt to help us always remember home," Anna's mother said. Follow this loving story of a simple quilt as it becomes a treasured family keepsake, passing traditions and stories from one generation to another.

READING CIRCLE

Bid students to join you for this sentimental story by singing this song to the tune of "She'll Be Comin' Round the Mountain."

> Come and read about a very special quilt.
> Come and read about a very special quilt.
> Anna's mother made it new.
> Now it's old and precious, too!
> Come and read about a very special quilt.

(Repeat the song until all your youngsters have gathered in your reading area.)

When students are settled in for storytime, share *The Keeping Quilt.*

 **LEARNING LINKS**

—Movement

After reading the story, revisit the illustrations. Can your students find all the ways the quilt was used? Keep track of their findings on a chart or on your chalkboard. Point out that the quilt was used as part of many weddings, and that people danced in celebration at these events. Then invite your little ones to form a circle and dance as you sing this song to the tune of "Mary Had a Little Lamb." Encourage your students to think of other movements to add to the song.

We will [dance] around the room, around the room,
    around the room.
We will [dance] around the room.
Come and [dance] with us!

Repeat the verse, substituting other movements—such as walk, hop, trot, *or* skip—*for the underlined words.*

71

PURPOSEFUL PLAY

ART SMARTS

Invite your little ones to help make a quilt to represent your classroom family. To prepare, bring in a twin-size sheet in a solid white or pastel. Purchase some transfer fabric crayons at your local craft or fabric store. Provide each child with a sheet of copy paper and instruct her to use the fabric crayons to draw a favorite animal. Tell them that the harder they press down as they draw with the crayons, the brighter the color on the finished quilt will be. As children are drawing, cover a table with a thick layer of newspaper, topped with a layer of plain white bulletin board paper. Then lay the sheet on top of the white paper. As a child finishes, have her lay her paper, drawing side down, on top of the sheet. Iron over the paper to make the drawing transfer onto the sheet (a teacher's job only, of course). When all the animal drawings have been transferred onto the sheet, your class will have made its very own keeping quilt!

Invite your classroom family to a Traditions Tea Party! Spread a tablecloth on the floor. Or, if you made a classroom family quilt (see "Art Smarts"), use that instead. Invite youngsters to sit around the edge of the cloth and sip some Russian Tea (see "Storybook Café"). As they drink their tea, talk about *family traditions*—things families do together in a special way. Do you have any classroom traditions? Maybe a Traditions Tea Party could be the first one!

STORYBOOK CAFÉ

Mix, stir, and sip at teatime!

Russian Tea

Supplies:
storage container
measuring spoons
measuring cup
mixing spoon
teakettle
Styrofoam® cups
plastic spoons

Ingredients:
1 cup Tang® drink mix
1/2 cup iced tea mix with lemon
1 1/2 cups sugar (or to taste)
1 tsp. cinnamon
1/2 tsp. ground cloves

To make Russian tea:
1. Measure and mix all the ingredients in the storage container.
2. Heat water in the teakettle.
3. Add three spoonfuls of Russian tea mix to a cup.
4. Pour in hot (not boiling) water. Stir.
5. Allow to cool before sipping.

SOMEBODY LOVES YOU, MR. HATCH

Written by Eileen Spinelli
Illustrated by Paul Yalowitz

A huge box of chocolates arrives, bringing Mr. Hatch some tasty treats and some big changes in his life.

READING CIRCLE

Call your youngsters to your reading circle by singing these verses to the tune of "The Wheels on the Bus."

Come meet a man named Mr. Hatch,
Mr. Hatch, Mr. Hatch.
Come meet a man named Mr. Hatch
In our reading circle.

Something's changed about Mr. Hatch,
Mr. Hatch, Mr. Hatch.
Something's changed about Mr. Hatch.
Come find out and see!

(Repeat the verses until all your students have joined you in the reading area.)

After your reading fans have gathered, read aloud *Somebody Loves You, Mr. Hatch.*

LEARNING LINKS

—Language Arts

School helpers will be just as surprised as Mr. Hatch when they receive personalized thank-you notes from your class. After sharing the story, discuss how Mr. Hatch begins acting more *neighborly,* or friendly, after receiving the mysterious chocolates. Enlist your group's help in listing the many neighborly people who help your school run smoothly: secretaries, administrators, cafeteria workers, school bus drivers, volunteers, and crossing guards. Then ask each child to remember something neighborly that someone on the list did for him. For each child, photocopy the thank-you note on page 75 onto light-colored construction paper. Help each youngster write the recipient's name on the top blank. Encourage him to write/dictate what that person did to help; then have him sign his name. Last, have him glue his photo next to the speech bubble. Invite each child to present his recipient with this special thank-you note. Surprise! Somebody loves you!

Somebody loves you, Mr. Simpson!
Thank you for
helping me get on the bus after school every day

Thanks!

Kara
(child's name)

ART SMARTS

Mr. Hatch helps his friends and neighbors in many ways. Ask the children to list some of their neighbors at home and school. Then have youngsters brainstorm ways they could help their neighbors. Invite each child to draw a picture showing one way she could help. Have her write/dictate a sentence about her illustration. Next have her create a frame for her work that Mr. Hatch would surely love! Provide shoelaces, paints, and colorful construction paper. Have each student dip one end of a shoelace into the paint. Put the wet lace on one side of the paper. Fold the other half of the paper on top of the shoelace. Press the paper down with one hand and pull out the shoelace with the other. Open the paper. Repeat these steps using other colors of paint. After the paint dries, mount your students' illustrations on the painted frames. Display the completed projects on a bulletin board titled "Nice and Neighborly!"

Denisha is my neighbor. She is only 3! I can show her how to jump rope.

Me — Just do this!
Denisha — OK!

Ashley 2-10-00

PURPOSEFUL PLAY

Youngsters will enjoy throwing their own party for Mr. Hatch in your dramatic-play area. Hang a banner that reads "Everybody Loves Mr. Hatch!" and stock an area of your classroom with items from the story, such as a picnic cloth, empty containers of candy, lengths of yellow streamers, paper hearts, bows, cooking supplies, plastic lemons, and empty boxes of brownie mix. Then let the celebration begin! At the close of center time, remind youngsters to take down all decorations so the next group will have the pleasure of preparing for Mr. Hatch's surprise party.

STORYBOOK CAFÉ

Mr. Hatch would no doubt recommend this easy-to-prepare candy recipe. Double the recipe, and your youngsters can share it with another class. How neighborly!

Friends-Stick-Together Chocolate Candy
(makes about 30 candies)

Ingredients:
12-oz. bag chocolate chips
10-oz. bag pretzel sticks

Supplies:
hot plate *or* microwave
heavy saucepan *or* microwave-safe bowl
metal spoon
waxed paper
cookie sheet

To make friends-stick-together chocolate candy:
1. Melt the chocolate chips in the saucepan over low heat or in the microwave for one to two minutes on high.
2. Stir in the pretzel sticks. Mix thoroughly, chopping some of the sticks with your spoon.
3. Drop by mounds onto a cookie sheet covered with waxed paper.
4. Chill until hardened, about one hour.

Use with "Learning Links" on page 73.

Somebody loves you, ______________________________!

Thank you for

Thanks!

____

____

____

______________________________.

____
(child's name)

Somebody loves you, ______________________________!

Thank you for

Thanks!

____

____

____

______________________________.

____
(child's name)

ROSE AND SEBASTIAN

Written by Cynthia Zarin
Illustrated by Sarah Durham

What's that scary noise? Join Rose as she transforms her fear into a new friendship with a nearby neighbor.

READING CIRCLE

Summon your young bookworms to the reading circle by singing this song to the tune of "Six White Ducks."

Come meet a girl whose name is Rose.
She heard some sounds that were very close.
What was the noise? Who made the shouts?
Come to the reading circle—you'll find out!
You'll find out! You'll find out!
Come to the reading circle—you'll find out!

(Repeat until all youngsters have joined the circle.)

Once your little ones have gathered, read the *first half* of *Rose and Sebastian.* See "Learning Links" for more details.

 # LEARNING LINKS

—Language Arts

This suspenseful story will capture the attention of your little book fans and provide opportunities for creative writing and some noisemaking! When you share this book with your class, stop reading when Rose knocks on Sebastian's door. Encourage each child to illustrate and write or dictate a conclusion to the story. Have each author share his page with the group; then finish reading the story. Then read the book a second time and encourage your youngsters to help you make all the noises that the city, Sebastian—and finally Rose—make. Did you ever think your reading circle could be so wonderfully noisy?

Sebastian is a giant with big boots that makes lots of noise! But he's nice.

Jared

ART SMARTS

The more you add to this bulletin board, the better it gets! Cut out several large apartment buildings from bulletin board paper. Cut out at least one window per child. Next, glue each child's class photo to a colored index card and mount it behind a window. Then encourage your little ones to visit your art center and create things they might see in a city, such as cars, trucks, dogs, people, and airplanes. Mount all their creations on the board. Add to the fun of this display by inviting each child to write or dictate a Sebastian-like noise on a conversation balloon to post near her photo.

PURPOSEFUL PLAY

Making noises can be fun—and figuring out what makes them can be, too! Sharpen your little ones' listening skills with this playful activity. Say the verse below for your little listeners. Then duck behind a screen or a desk as you make a noise, such as crumpling paper, ringing a bell, closing a desk drawer, clapping your hands, or blowing a whistle. Pop back out and invite a student volunteer to identify the sound he heard. Then keep going with more nifty noises!

> Can you hear it?
> Listen closely,
> Listen with each ear.
>
> Can you guess
> What makes this sound?
> Please tell me what you hear!

STORYBOOK CAFÉ

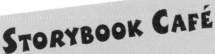

Youngsters will certainly make noise as they devour this crunchy snack!

Crunchy Munchies
(serves 20)

Supplies:
large bowl
large spoon for mixing
measuring cup
small paper plates

Ingredients:
two 6-oz. packages tiny fish-shaped crackers
2 cups oyster crackers
1½ cups thin pretzel sticks, broken in half
1 cup mixed nuts

To make crunchy munchies:
1. Pour all ingredients into the bowl.
2. Stir gently and serve in half-cup portions.
3. Crunch it and munch it!

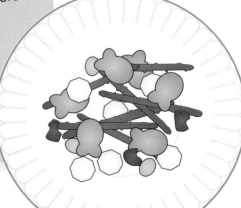

77

MAMA PROVI AND THE POT OF RICE

Written by Sylvia Rosa-Casanova
Illustrated by Robert Roth

Join Mama Provi as she climbs the stairs in her apartment building. Along the way she'll meet some neighbors and show your little ones what sharing is all about!

READING CIRCLE

Your reading enthusiasts will eagerly join your reading circle when you sing this verse to the tune of "The Itsy Bitsy Spider."

Come and meet a grandma who cooks a pot of rice.
In goes some chicken and then a little spice.
Up goes the grandma to climb a lot of stairs,
But you'll have to join our circle to find out
    why she cares!

(Repeat until everyone has joined the circle.)

Once your little ones have gathered for storytime, read aloud *Mama Provi and the Pot of Rice.*

LEARNING LINKS

—Language Arts

Each of your students will be eager to dramatize her own version of *Mama Provi and the Pot of Rice* when she completes this nifty activity. Invite each child to cut photos of five favorite foods from magazines. Have her glue each cutout to a separate small paper plate. Ask her to write or dictate the name of each food on the plate and then to decorate the edge of each plate with markers or crayons. Provide each child with a paper lunch bag that has been programmed with the phrase "_____ and the Pot of _____." Ask each child to write her name on the first blank and then to select one of her food choices to be written on the second blank. Then have her place her plates in the bag. Cook up some fun by encouraging each child to retell the story using the foods in her own bag.

78

—Math

How many food fans in your class would taste each of the items in Mama Provi's bag? In advance, use a permanent marker to write each child's name on the handle of a plastic fork. Then prepare a yes/no tabletop graph and a tagboard chart listing the foods from the story. Review each food Mama Provi has in her bag. Distribute the forks; then ask your group, "Would you taste chicken and rice?" Instruct each child to place her fork in the column representing her response. Chorally count the forks in each column and record the results on the chart. Return the forks to their owners and continue to survey your group about each food from the story. Afterward, discuss all the results. Hot-glue the forks around the edge of the chart for a delicious display.

PURPOSEFUL PLAY

Give your group a taste of some neighborly trading with this role-playing activity. Ask for volunteers to role-play Mama Provi and four of her neighbors. Provide "Mama Provi" with a shopping bag containing five small snack bags filled with dried rice. Give each of the neighbors two snack bags filled with one of the following: dried black beans, half slices of bread, tea bags, and apple slices. Have Mama Provi visit each of her neighbors and trade one snack bag of rice for one snack bag of theirs. When the role-playing is finished, point out that each of the neighbors now has two different foods and Mama Provi has several different foods! Continue role-playing until all your students have had a chance to participate.

STORYBOOK CAFÉ

Use crispy rice cereal to make this dish that Mama Provi would love!

Mama Provi's Crispy Rice Crunchers
(makes approximately 24)

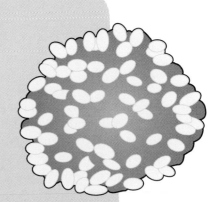

Supplies:
mixing bowl
waxed paper
resealable plastic bag
large spoon
measuring cup

Ingredients:
1 cup peanut butter
$\frac{1}{4}$ cup chopped nuts
$\frac{3}{4}$ cup dried milk
$\frac{3}{4}$ cup chocolate-covered raisins
1 cup crispy rice cereal

To make crispy rice crunchers:
1. Mix peanut butter, nuts, dried milk, and chocolate-covered raisins in the bowl. Add a little more dried milk if your mixture is too wet.
2. Pour some crispy rice cereal into a resealable plastic bag.
3. Put a spoonful of the peanut butter mixture on a square of waxed paper.
4. Roll the mixture into a ball.
5. Shake the ball in the bag with the cereal.
6. Repeat Steps 2–5 until you've used up all the peanut butter mixture.

IF SOMEBODY LIVED NEXT DOOR

Written by Libby Hough
Illustrated by Laura McGee Kvasnosky

A little girl's imagination fills the empty house next door with some very interesting neighbors.

READING CIRCLE

Round up your youngsters for storytime by singing this verse to the tune of "A-Tisket A-Tasket."

A neighbor, a neighbor,
Olivia needs a neighbor.
The house next door is empty.
She has no one to play with.
To play with, to play with,
She has no one to play with.
Come join our circle, come sit down,
To see what she will do!

(Repeat until all the children have joined the circle.)

Once all your little ones have joined the reading circle, read aloud *If Somebody Lived Next Door.*

 **LEARNING LINKS**

—Language Arts

Whom would your little thinkers wish to have as next-door neighbors? For each child, draw a large thought bubble on a 12" x 18" sheet of manila paper; then program it with the text shown. After reading the book, ask each student to pretend the house next door to his is empty. What kind of neighbors might move in? Invite each child to create a portrait of these imaginary neighbors inside his thought bubble. Encourage him to write or dictate to complete the sentence. Then glue a photo of the child in the bottom corner. During circle time, have each child share his work. Then mount the completed projects on a bulletin board titled "Who Would Live Next Door to You?"

Aaron 3/26/00

Butterflies
___BtrfiS___ would live next door to
they make a rainbow when they fly
me because __mK a rnbo fli__.

I would plant a butterfly bush and watch the butterflies every day. They would float over and say, "Let's play, Aaron!"

Aaron

80

—Social Skills

At the end of the story, someone really does move in next door to Olivia. Ask youngsters to brainstorm what Olivia might say when she meets her new neighbor. After discussing student ideas, lead youngsters to conclude that Olivia needs to introduce herself. Have a child role-play the new neighbor while you pretend to be Olivia. Think aloud as you model for youngsters how to introduce yourself:

1. First think, "Is this a good time to introduce myself, or is the other person busy?"
2. Walk up to the person, but don't get *too* close!
3. Smile!
4. Say, "Hello, my name is…"
5. Then wait to see if the other person responds with her name. If she doesn't, then ask, "What is your name?"

Ask for student volunteers to role-play introducing themselves to someone in front of the group; then have all youngsters find a partner and practice this important social skill.

PURPOSEFUL PLAY

As Olivia plays with her farm toys, she imagines that they become her new next-door neighbors. Spark your student's imaginations each day by stocking your block center with different types of plastic/stuffed animals for several days. For example, provide farm animals one day, zoo animals the following day, and dinosaurs the day after that. Encourage youngsters to use the blocks to build Olivia's house and the empty house next door. Now, what kind of animals will be Olivia's neighbors today?

STORYBOOK CAFÉ

These easy-to-fix treats are a great way to welcome a new neighbor!

Howdy, Neighbors!

Supplies:
craft sticks
small paper plates
toaster

Ingredients:
1 slice of raisin bread per child
1 cup peanut butter for every 15 children
1 tbsp. miniature semisweet chocolate chips per child

To make one howdy, neighbor:
1. Toast a slice of raisin bread.
2. Use a craft stick to spread peanut butter on the toast.
3. Make a smiling face with the chocolate chips.
4. Mmmm…howdy, neighbor!

LOUDMOUTH GEORGE AND THE NEW NEIGHBORS

Written & Illustrated by Nancy Carlson

George is sure he doesn't want to be friends with the new family of pigs next door. Or is he?

READING CIRCLE

Invite little ones to join your reading circle by singing these verses to the tune of "Ten Little Indians."

Loudmouth George has brand-new neighbors.
Loudmouth George has brand-new neighbors.
Loudmouth George has brand-new neighbors
Living right next door!

Come find out what George will do.
Come find out what George will do.
Come find out what George will do
In our reading circle!

(Repeat until all your students have joined the circle.)

When your students are quiet and ready to hear the story, read aloud *Loudmouth George and the New Neighbors.*

 ## LEARNING LINKS

—Science

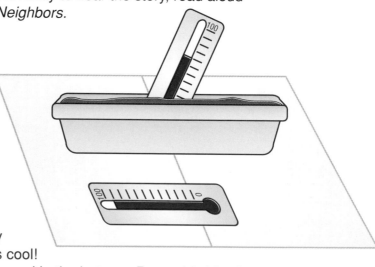

Louanne gets a bad rap when it comes to being a pig. George thinks she is dirty before he even meets her! Actually, pigs keep beds of straw cleaner than horses or cows do. Pigs *do* like to wallow in the mud; that's probably the reason George thinks pigs are dirty animals. But for a pig, wallowing in mud isn't dirty—it's cool! Explain that pigs know that lying in mud will keep them cool in the hot sun. Prove this idea by mixing up a batch of ooey-gooey mud in a large foil pan. Next, lay two thermometers side by side on a warm sidewalk. After students confirm that both thermometers show the same degree of temperature, nestle one into the mud. Leave the other thermometer on the sidewalk. After a few minutes, check the mud-covered thermometer. Youngsters will be pleased to find that the temperature reading has been lowered by the mud. Those pigs! They're not only clean—but smart, too!

ART SMARTS

Your little ones will enjoy creating and reading this eye-popping book full of neighborly introductions. Encourage each child to draw a self-portrait on a copy of page 84 and then glue a pair of large wiggle eyes in place. Ask each child to write her name on the blank line. Punch holes along the left margin and put the pages in a three-ring binder titled "Classroom Neighbors All Around." Share the completed book with your group; then tell students that the order of the pages will be changed each day. Youngsters will be sure to pick up this book every day to discover who their new neighbors are!

Theme: NEIGHBORS
Class Book Page
Use with "Art Smarts" on page 83.

Hello! My name is ___Katie___.
How are you today?
Turn the page and you'll find out
Who my neighbor is today!

PURPOSEFUL PLAY

George's friends, Harriet and Ralph, go right over to meet his new neighbors. Encourage your children to practice introducing themselves by playing a game of "Hello!" Sit in a circle with a small group of children. Have one child roll a ball across the circle to another child in the group and say, "Hello! My name is [child's name]. How are you today?" Ask the child receiving the ball to respond, "I'm fine! My name is [child's name]." Continue the game by having the child who received the ball become the "roller" and introduce himself as he rolls the ball to another child.

STORYBOOK CAFÉ

George can't resist playing in the sprinkler with his friends, and your little ones won't be able to resist this snack made with sure-to-make-you-smile sprinkles!

Sprinkled Circles

Supplies:
plastic knives or craft sticks
napkins

Ingredients:
round, buttery crackers (3 per child)
soft cream cheese
sprinkles

To make sprinkled circles:
1. Spread cream cheese on a cracker.
2. Add sprinkles.
3. Repeat and eat!

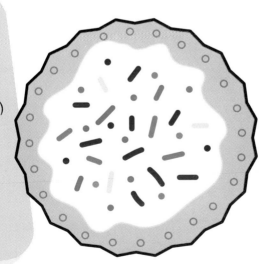

Hello! My name is _____.

How are you today?

Turn the page and you'll find out

Who my neighbor is today!

GUESS WHO?

Written & Photo-Illustrated by Margaret Miller

Butcher, baker, or candlestick maker? Guess which community helper is hiding behind each page of this fun-filled book!

READING CIRCLE

Guess who's coming to your reading circle? It'll be your students when you sing this musical invitation to the tune of "Where Is Thumbkin?"!

Who does this job? Who does that job?
Can you guess? Can you guess?
Let's all read this guessing book
In our reading circle!
Come join me! Come join me!

(Repeat until all your little guessers have gathered in your reading area.)

Once your little ones are settled, read aloud *Guess Who?*

LEARNING LINKS

—Math

What makes a person a community helper? How are they different from other workers? Your youngsters will discover the differences with this graphing activity. In advance, draw a line to divide a large sheet of chart paper into two columns. Label one side "Community Helpers" and the other side "Other Workers." Discuss each worker in Margaret Miller's book; then select a student to illustrate and label an index card for each worker (or do this yourself as younger students watch). Ask a student volunteer to decide which category each card belongs in. Remind students that community helpers work to provide things we all need, such as safety, shelter, food, or health care. Affix the cards to the chart to create a graph. Together, count the cards in each column. Were there more community helpers or other workers in the story?

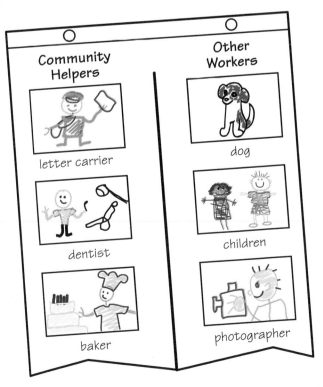

Art Smarts

You never know who may pop up in this activity! To prepare, duplicate page 87 for each child. Invite each child in a small group to color and then cut out the five community helpers. Have him also cut out the poem box. Then provide each student with three straws and a small Styrofoam® cup. Read the poem together; then have each child tape the poem box around the outside of his cup. Have him cut the three straws in half and discard one of the halves. Have him tape one community helper cutout to each remaining straw. Direct each child to push one straw through the bottom of his cup to make a hole. To use the pop-up, a child inserts one community helper straw into the cup so that it is hidden. He recites the poem and gives a clue about the helper. After the other children in the group guess, he pushes the straw up so that the community helper pops up for all to see!

Purposeful Play

Invite youngsters to dress the part of community helpers in your dramatic-play area. Gather a variety of simple clothing items and props that little ones can use to dress as workers from the book, such as aprons, cooking utensils, toy tools, a toy medical kit, a canvas tote bag and a collection of discarded junk mail, and a toy camera. Also include any career hats you have as well as a full-length mirror. Encourage each visitor at the center to dress up and invite playmates to guess her occupation.

Storybook Café

Your youngsters will love taking on the role of baker as they prepare these tasty pretzel treats.

Baker's Pretzels
(makes 8)

Supplies:
cookie sheet
knife
pastry brush

Ingredients:
1 loaf of frozen bread dough, thawed
flour
2 tbsp. butter or margarine, melted
salt

To make baker's pretzels:
1. Slice the dough into eight equal portions.
2. Flour your hands; then roll and stretch each portion of dough into a long strip (about 12 to 18 inches long).
3. Crisscross the strip to form a pretzel shape.
4. Place the pretzels on the cookie sheet and brush with margarine.
5. Sprinkle with salt.
6. Bake at 350 degrees for 25 minutes or until light golden brown.

Theme: COMMUNITY HELPERS

Community Helper Patterns
Use with "Art Smarts" on page 86.

carpenter   **doctor**   **police officer**   **baker**   **letter carrier**

Poem
Use with "Art Smarts" on page 86.

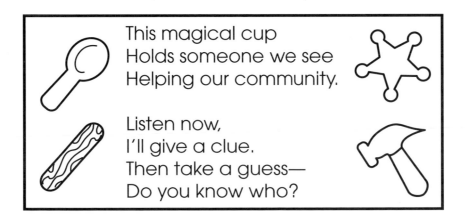

This magical cup
Holds someone we see
Helping our community.

Listen now,
I'll give a clue.
Then take a guess—
Do you know who?

WORK

Written by Ann Morris

Come and meet workers from around our world. You'll discover they're a lot like you and me!

READING CIRCLE

Gather your students together for reading time with this song sung to the tune of "Row, Row, Row Your Boat."

Join me on a trip,
Around the world we'll look.
Reading circle is the place.
It's all in this great book!

We'll meet workers and
See just what they do.
Reading circle is the place.
So join me, please, won't you?

(Repeat the verses until all your youngsters have worked their way to the reading area.)

Once your students are ready to read, share *Work*.

 **LEARNING LINKS**

—Social Studies

This display will show off workers everywhere! Title a large bulletin board "People Work." Divide the board into three sections labeled "At Home," "In Our Community," and "Around the World." Encourage each child to illustrate a picture for one category; then write his dictation about his drawing. Help him place his drawing on the board in the appropriate area.

ART SMARTS

Encourage your little ones to explore a variety of career paths with this mat-making activity. For each child, program a 12" x 18" sheet of colorful construction paper as shown. Then have each child cut out magazine photos of people doing jobs that he finds interesting. Glue a child's photo in the center of his mat; then have the child glue the magazine photos in the open space on the mat. After discussing each child's career interests, send these mats home to become keepsakes for moms and dads.

There are so many things that I can be...

Take a look at some jobs that interest me!

PURPOSEFUL PLAY

Reinforce the fact that the world is a busy place with this idea for playtime. Divide your class into several groups and give each group a different set of play props, such as puppets, blocks, play dough, and dress-up costumes. Allow youngsters to play in their groups for 15 minutes. Then regroup and ask a child to describe what was going on in all the other groups. If he finds this nearly impossible to do, point out that your classroom is a miniature version of the world—people everywhere are working at many different tasks. What a busy place our planet is!

STORYBOOK CAFÉ

Try this snack that combines work and play—and eating, too! Youngsters will work to create it, play with it, and then eat it up!

Edible Play Dough
(makes 15 portions)

Supplies:
large mixing bowl
mixing spoon
waxed paper
measuring cups

Ingredients:
$1^3/_4$ cups peanut butter
2 cups powdered sugar
$1^3/_4$ cups honey
2 cups powdered milk

To make edible play dough:
1. Combine all ingredients in a large bowl.
2. Stir the mixture until it forms a dough.
3. Place a portion of dough on a square of waxed paper. Knead it until it achieves a play dough consistency.
4. Play and eat!

OFFICER BUCKLE AND GLORIA

Written & Illustrated by Peggy Rathmann

We all know that a police officer is a community helper, but in this book there's a crazy canine that's doing an important job, too!

READING CIRCLE

Call your young reading hounds to the reading circle with this song sung to the tune of "Old MacDonald."

> Officer Buckle had a dog
> And Gloria was her name.
>
> With a bark, bark here
> And a bark, bark there.
> Here a bark, there a bark,
> Everywhere a bark, bark!
>
> Come meet her in our reading circle.
> You'll be glad you came!

(Repeat until all youngsters have gathered in your reading area.)

Once everyone is settled in to hear a story, read aloud *Officer Buckle and Gloria.*

 ## LEARNING LINKS

—Social Studies

Take a tip from Officer Buckle and make these safety stars to remind little ones about school safety. In advance, cut out a class supply of large construction paper stars. Then divide your class into groups. Ask each group to think of tips for a particular area of school safety, such as playground safety, classroom safety, or bus safety. Ask each child to illustrate and write/dictate one tip from the group's brainstormed list. Display the finished safety stars in your classroom or the hallway. Then follow the stars to safety!

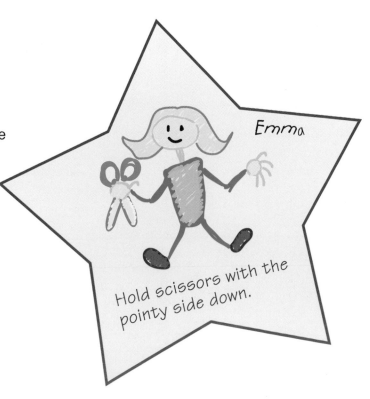

Emma

Hold scissors with the pointy side down.

—Problem Solving

Put your young detectives to work on the case of the missing dog! Prior to this activity, hide a stuffed dog somewhere on your playground. Then create a set of clues, leading detectives from one place to another, including a final clue that will lead them to the dog's location. Hide the clue cards in the appropriate locations. Compose a letter from Officer Buckle explaining that Gloria is missing and that he needs their help. Include the first clue card with the letter. Then set your little detectives on the trail. Imagine how proud they'll be when they crack this case!

Dear Boys and Girls,

Help! Gloria is missing! Can you help me find her? Here is a clue to help you.

Officer Buckle

Look under the slide.

PURPOSEFUL PLAY

Are your students as good at acting out safety tips as Gloria? Find out with a game of Safety Charades. Whisper a safety tip from the story into a youngster's ear; then have her act it out for the class. Can they guess the tip?

STORYBOOK CAFÉ

Your little ones will love sharing this canine treat with a favorite doggie friend!

Doggie Bones
(makes approximately 20 small bones)

Supplies:
large mixing bowl
cookie sheet
large spoon
measuring cups
measuring spoons

Ingredients:
$1\frac{1}{2}$ cups flour
$\frac{1}{3}$ cup milk
$\frac{1}{3}$ cup beef bouillon or chicken broth
1 tsp. salt
2 tbsp. butter (softened)
2 tsp. baking powder

To make doggie bones:
1. Mix all ingredients to form a dough.
2. Place the dough on a lightly floured surface and knead the dough several times.
3. Shape a portion of the dough into a bone shape.
4. Place the doggie bone on a cookie sheet.
5. Bake in a 400-degree oven for 20 to 25 minutes or until browned.

BUSY PEOPLE

Written & Illustrated by Nick Butterworth

Community helpers are busy, busy, busy in this book about all kinds of jobs.

READING CIRCLE

Invite your little ones to the reading circle with this sing-along to the tune of "The Farmer in the Dell."

It's time for reading circle.
It's time for reading circle.
Come read this book and take a look
At all the busy people!

A carpenter builds a house.
A carpenter builds a house.
Come read this book and take a look
At all the busy people!

A baker bakes some bread.
A baker bakes some bread.
Come read this book and take a look
At all the busy people!

(Encourage student volunteers to name other community helpers for additional verses. Continue singing until all the children have gathered in your reading area.)

Once everyone is settled, read aloud *Busy People.*

LEARNING LINKS

—Social Studies

Have youngsters work cooperatively to create these kid-sized community helpers. Divide your class into small groups of three to four children. Provide each group with a long length of bulletin board paper, crayons, scissors, construction paper, and glue. Assign each group a community helper and explain how to create it. Have one child in each group lay faceup on the bulletin board paper as another child traces around his body. Have another child cut out the helper on the outline. (Provide assistance for younger children.) Then have all the group members use the crayons, paper, scissors, and glue to draw or make features, clothing, and/or tools for the helper. Display the completed helpers around your classroom, along with sentence-strip labels so visitors can identify each of these very special workers!

—Sensory Perception

This center activity will have little ones using their sense of touch and their brain power, too! Onto each of several canisters, attach a picture of a different community helper. (If desired, use the community helper patterns on page 87.) Place the canisters on a table, along with a small tool or item associated with each helper. For example, use a wooden spoon for a chef, a tongue depressor for a doctor, or a toy badge for a police officer. Invite students to visit the center in pairs. Have one child wear a blindfold. Have the other child examine one canister at a time. Have him announce the name of the community helper. The blindfolded child then feels each object on the table, determines which item goes with the named helper, and hands it to her partner. The partner places the chosen item in the canister and continues with another canister. Have the guesser remove her blindfold and check her accuracy. Then have the two switch places and repeat the activity.

PURPOSEFUL PLAY

Ready…set…dress! Little ones will be scrambling into community helper costumes with this fun relay! Arrange two community helper costumes in separate boxes. The costumes may be different, as long as they have an equal number of items. Divide your class into two teams, and have each team line up one child behind another. Place a costume box at the front of each line. Give a starting signal and have the first child in each line begin to put on the costume. Once he's dressed, he undresses again and hands the costume to the next child in line. Then he goes to the back of the line. The first team to have all its members try on the costume wins!

STORYBOOK CAFÉ

Revisit the page of *Busy People* that shows Sally the clothier. Then invite youngsters to get busy making this fashionable fare!

Sally's T-shirt Toasts

Supplies:
table knife
paper plates
plastic knives

Ingredients for one child:
1 slice toast
peanut butter
jelly
raisins
bananas (peeled and sliced)

To make one T-shirt toast:
1. Trim the slice of toast into a T-shirt shape.
2. Spread peanut butter or jelly on the T-shirt toast.
3. Use raisins and banana pieces to create a unique T-shirt design.

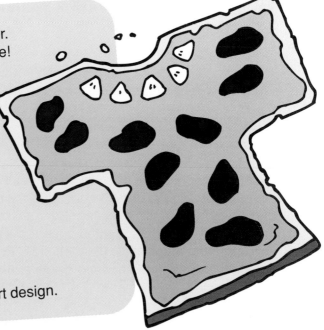

WHOSE HAT?

Written & Photo-Illustrated by Margaret Miller

Tall hats, short hats, hard hats, too! Can you guess which hat is whose?

 ## READING CIRCLE

Round up your youngsters for reading time with this song sung to the tune of "Twinkle, Twinkle, Little Star."

Come and read this book with me.
Oh, how many hats you'll see!

Hard hats, soft hats, hats you use—
Try and guess whose hat is whose!

Come and read this book with me.
Oh, how many hats you'll see!

(Repeat until all your youngsters have gathered in the reading circle.)

When everyone is ready to read, share *Whose Hat?*

 ## LEARNING LINKS

—Language Arts

Your youngsters will flip over these community helper flip books. In advance, take a close-up photo of each child and have the film developed. Cut around each child's head and shoulders. Then mount the cropped photo on a 4" x 6" piece of tagboard as shown. Duplicate the booklet pages on page 96 for each child to color. Have each youngster cut apart the boxes. Direct him to glue the page with the final sentence above his photo. Then have him stack the remaining pages and cover on top of the last page, and staple along the left side. Encourage him to flip through the pages to discover the many hats he may want to wear in life.

ART SMARTS

Make these paper firefighter helmets for all your future firefighters to wear. To prepare, fold a class supply of red construction paper in half lengthwise. Use a black marker to draw two lines as shown. Direct each child to begin cutting at the fold and follow the lines until they end. Then have her snip off the top and bottom corners that are not on the fold (through both thicknesses of paper). Have her unfold the paper. Label the brim of each child's hat as shown. Then provide her with yellow paint to create an emblem or shield in the center. When the paint is dry, show her how to pop up the cutout center to form a hat. And it's ready to wear!

PURPOSEFUL PLAY

Pass the hat! Youngsters will be eager to join the fun with this musical game. Seat youngsters in a circle. Put on some lively music and begin passing a community helper's hat (such as a hard hat). The child holding the hat when you stop the music is out. Continue playing and passing until only one player remains. Be sure to have a fun activity for children to go to as they are eliminated from the game. Maybe they could head over to the snack table to make the following recipe!

3"

6"

Firefighter Abby

STORYBOOK CAFÉ

Top off your day with this nutritious snack!

Healthy Hard Hat Sundae

Supplies:
plastic bowls
plastic spoons
ice-cream scoop
table knife (for cutting grapes)

Ingredients for each child:
1 scoop vanilla frozen yogurt
1 canned peach half
1 grape half
raisins

To make a healthy hard hat sundae:
1. Place a scoop of frozen yogurt in a bowl.
2. Top the yogurt with a peach half (a hard hat).
3. Add raisin eyes, a grape-half nose, and a raisin smile.

Booklet Pages
Use with "Learning Links" on page 94.

When I grow up,
what will I be?

_____
Name

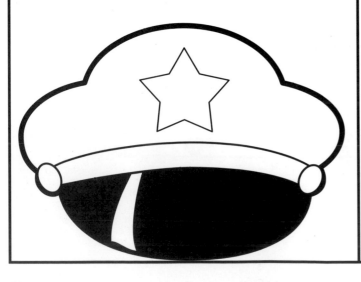

I guess I'll
have to
wait and see!